The Reemergence of Liberation Theologies

New Approaches to Religion and Power

Series editor: Joerg Rieger

While the relationship of religion and power is a perennial topic, it only continues to grow in importance and scope in our increasingly globalized and diverse world. Religion, on a global scale, has openly joined power struggles, often in support of the powers that be. But at the same time, religion has made major contributions to resistance movements. In this context, current methods in the study of religion and theology have created a deeper awareness of the issue of power: critical theory, cultural studies, postcolonial theory, subaltern studies, feminist theory, critical race theory, and working class studies are contributing to a new quality of study in the field. This series is a place for both studies of particular problems in the relation of religion and power as well as for more general interpretations of this relation. It undergirds the growing recognition that religion can no longer be studied without the study of power.

Series editor:

Joerg Rieger is Wendland-Cook Professor of Constructive Theology in the Perkins School of Theology at Southern Methodist University.

Titles:

*No Longer the Same: Religious Others and the Liberation of
    Christian Theology*
David R. Brockman

*The Subject, Capitalism, and Religion: Horizons of Hope in
    Complex Societies*
Jung Mo Sung

Imaging Religion in Film: The Politics of Nostalgia
M. Gail Hamner

*Spaces of Modern Theology: Geography and Power in
    Schleiermacher's World*
Steven R. Jungkeit

*Transcending Greedy Money: Interreligious Solidarity for
    Just Relations*
Ulrich Duchrow and Franz J. Hinkelammert

*Foucault, Douglass, Fanon, and Scotus in Dialogue:
    On Social Construction and Freedom*
Cynthia R. Nielsen

Lenin, Religion, and Theology
Roland Boer

*In Search of God's Power in Broken Bodies:
    A Theology of Maum*
Hwa-Young Chong

*The Reemergence of Liberation Theologies: Models for the
    Twenty-First Century*
Edited by Thia Cooper

The Reemergence of Liberation Theologies
Models for the Twenty-First Century

Edited by
Thia Cooper

palgrave
macmillan

THE REEMERGENCE OF LIBERATION THEOLOGIES
Copyright © Thia Cooper, 2013.

First published in 2013 by
PALGRAVE MACMILLAN®
in the United States—a division of St. Martin's Press LLC,
175 Fifth Avenue, New York, NY 10010.

Where this book is distributed in the UK, Europe and the rest of the world,
this is by Palgrave Macmillan, a division of Macmillan Publishers Limited,
registered in England, company number 785998, of Houndmills,
Basingstoke, Hampshire RG21 6XS.

Palgrave Macmillan is the global academic imprint of the above companies
and has companies and representatives throughout the world.

Palgrave® and Macmillan® are registered trademarks in the United States,
the United Kingdom, Europe and other countries.

ISBN: 978–1–137–29244–5 (paperback)
ISBN: 978–1–137–30505–3 (hardcover)

Library of Congress Cataloging-in-Publication Data

The reemergence of liberation theologies : models for the
twenty-first century / Thia Cooper, ed.
        pages cm
    ISBN 978–1–137–30505–3 (hardcover : alk. paper)—
    ISBN 978–1–137–29244–5 (pbk. : alk. paper)
    1. Liberation theology. I. Cooper, Thia.
BT83.57.R44 2013
230′.0464—dc23   2013001813

A catalogue record of the book is available from the British Library.

Design by Newgen Imaging Systems (P) Ltd., Chwennai, India.

First edition: July 2013

10 9 8 7 6 5 4 3 2 1

This book is dedicated to Marcella Althaus-Reid and Ada María Isasi Díaz.

Contents

Part III Around the World

Part IV Practice

Part V Future

Acknowledgments

I would like to thank each of the contributors for their commitment to producing this volume. I also want to thank Ivan Petrella for his help and support in the first few years of the Liberation Theologies Consultation. I would like to thank each of the people who have attended and supported the consultation. I am delighted that there is a place for us to talk about liberation in the American Academy of Religion. I am grateful to the American Academy of Religion for approving our group. And finally, I am grateful to Gustavus Adolphus College for giving me a sabbatical that enabled me to work on this project.

Introduction

Thia Cooper

When I decided I wanted to study liberation theology in 1997, the overwhelming response from people I knew in the United States was, "Why would you want to research that? Liberation theology is dead." Apparently, it was dying in the 1980s, and with the fall of the Berlin Wall, it became a piece of history. I persevered anyway and found many theologies of liberation to be alive and well across the globe. This book shares with you a glimpse of some of the varieties of liberation theologies today.

Liberation theology is both action and reflection that aims to liberate marginalized peoples from oppression, to act. It argues that faith and religion should free people rather than oppress them, free them to act justly. At its beginnings, liberation theology emphasized that God is present now, working in the world through human beings. Further, God is on the side of the poor, opposing oppression. Salvation is not solely a spiritual concept, but it has a material component too. So too does sin, which exists in structures and in individuals. Sin is any form of injustice. The central value of salvation is justice. And this struggle for justice is to bring about a new heaven and a new earth. Many of these themes continue to be emphasized today in liberation theologies and new ones have arisen.

Liberation theology emerged in the 1960s in Catholic communities in Brazil and across Latin America as Christians worked to counter economic and political poverty. The majority of these countries' citizens lived in economic poverty. As the 1960s progressed many of these countries were taken over by their militaries through coups that replaced democratically elected governments with dictatorships (called National Security Regimes). Latin American citizens, then, lived in political poverty too, unable to participate in their political systems.

Many Latin American Christians began to speak out and act against both forms of poverty. Small communities of Christians, known as base ecclesial communities, formed. These communities met to discuss the Bible and their lives. The participants tended to be poor, church-related, and focused on community rather than the individual. Together, they struggled to survive in this poverty.

Toward the end of this decade, in 1968, Latin American bishops met in Medellín, Colombia, to respond to Vatican II, and they supported this emerging theology. It continued to spread and reached academic circles and the United States and Europe. The first book in English on liberation theology was published in 1974 by Gustavo Gutiérrez[1] titled *A Theology of Liberation*. During the 1970s, liberation theologies emerged in a variety of contexts around the world—in Africa, Asia, Europe, and across the Americas.[2]

In the early 1980s, as theologies of liberation continued to take root and expand, struggling against oppression in Latin America and beyond, Cardinal Joseph Ratzinger, who later became Pope, began to speak out against the theologies. Pope John Paul II silenced Catholic liberation theologians, such as Brazilian priest Leonardo Boff, for their writings. The Catholic hierarchy disapproved of theologies emerging from the people rather than the Pope; the hierarchy of the church was primary. Further, the church feared a turn to atheism as liberation theologians often supported socialist economic policies and socialism, which according to Pope John Paul II went hand in hand with atheism. This, however, was not the case in Latin America.

At the same time, governments across Latin America slowly began to return to democratic rule. At the end of the 1980s, with the fall of the Berlin Wall, it appeared to the global North (United States and Europe) that democratic capitalism had won and would expand across the globe through globalization. Socialism and communism were deemed to have failed. Many people in the global North assumed liberation theology was no longer necessary. It disappeared from the academy and as a discussion topic in many churches. And so, "it died."

Except it did not die. It regrouped to deal with the still oppressive situation. Economic and political poverty continued now under democratic capitalism rather than dictatorial capitalism. Liberation theologies have been active in many contexts, although ignored in the academy and many churches. Theologies of liberation expanded out from the Latin American liberation theology of the Catholic Church[4] to other forms of Christianity, and liberation theologies have emerged in other religious traditions. They address economic and political poverty, as well as gender inequality, racial inequality, sexual inequality, and so forth. This struggling occurs in a variety of settings around the world as this book shows.

Oppression did not disappear with the fall of the Berlin Wall. Liberationists still work against oppression. Many types of liberation theologies have been labeled contextual theologies and granted academic niches. Rather than examining the varieties of oppression together, how they overlap and intersect, it became racial oppression versus gender inequality versus ecological oppression and so forth. Particularities are very important. However, rather than showing that liberation theologies are overturning traditional theology, each one seems still atomized, given a small space on the margins to exist, competing with each other for that small space. In the academic setting, liberation theology as its own topic seemed absent, even at the American Academy of Religion (AAR), the guild for scholars of Religious Studies and Theology. Instead, a variety of theologians working on specific themes within liberation networked and presented in their niches, but nothing brought us together. We had to decide between womanist (African-American feminist) theology, mujerista (Latina feminist) theology, Latin American and Caribbean theologies, and so forth. There was no space to examine the overlaps between many of them.

Liberation theology has slowly returned to the academy in the United States and Europe as recognition spreads that it is still alive. In 2006, Marcella Althaus-Reid, a feminist and sexual theologian; Ivan Petrella, working in liberation theology and public policy; and I put a panel together for the AAR's Annual Conference focused on liberation theologies for the twenty-first century. Hundreds of people attended this session and a new group emerged that thrives today.

This book is the first fruit of our collaboration. What we hold in common are two themes. First, we work to cross borders of disciplines, of contexts, and wherever walls have been built. Second, we aim not to be a niche within theology but to transform theology itself into liberating rather than oppressive practices. Liberation theologies need to talk with each other and act together. And in truth some of us need to be liberated from our own oppressive practices.

Each of the pieces included in this book come from talks presented at the Annual Meeting of the American Academy of Religion, 2007–2011, in the first years of the Liberation Theologies Consultation. We have tried to keep them as brief and informal as they were at the meeting. We have, however, added notes and further explanations where necessary.

These contributions are just a few of the voices from the global North and South, presenting brief analyses of liberation theology's future. Each of these pieces is a sample of work in the field of liberation theology. Each is a starting point for further discussion. These authors ask: How can liberation theologies make a difference in this century? What are they doing? Where should they be going?

There are at least five unique features of this book. First, it is collaborative. The book brings together a variety of scholars and practitioners of liberation theologies to show its breadth and depth. There are many overlaps in the work of these authors. Second, it brings together established and new voices from those who began working in the 1970s all the way through to the voices emerging today. These newer voices build on the work of the first liberationists, using and adjusting the scaffolding. Third, this book contains an all-star cast from decades prior through today. If you are drawn to the book because of chapters by prominent theologians like Rosemary Radford Ruether or Emilie Townes, you will be enriched by many of the other scholars and issues addressed here. In addition, this book brings liberation theologies into the twenty-first century by including some of the rising stars. And finally, this book attempts to model the intersection of theory and practice. Each essay contains both and we have a specific section on practice. You can see the emergence and spread of liberation from its beginnings to now in the works that these theologians and practitioners cite and in the areas in which they work.

The liberation theologians and activists included work on a range of issues and use a variety of sources. These include biblical texts, theologians, social scientists, scientists, life experience, and so forth. We see work with indigenous populations in India, Mexico, the United States, and New Zealand; and feminist theologies, sexual theologies, black theologies, economic theologies, and political theologies. We have the voices of a womanist, a Korean Brazilian, and a Latino Canadian. We read about genocide, the drug trade on the US-Mexico border, and the oppression of American Indians and Palestinians. We see that artistic expression is becoming an important aspect of liberation theologies. And in case this does not seem like enough liberating work to take forward, there are plenty of other areas that need to be further developed, perhaps in another volume! Four that spring to mind are ecotheology, queer theology, sexual theology, and liberation theology within other religious traditions. Liberation theology continues to emerge in a variety of areas.

The book is divided into five sections, addressing the overall state of liberation theologies, the United States, other parts of the world, practice, and the future.

1. Does liberation theology matter for this century? Each author argues that it does. Dwight Hopkins argues that "imperial peace" is a contradiction in terms. He contrasts the notion of stewardship of creation with the imperial notions of private ownership and individualism. Joerg Rieger understands context as our shared pain rather than special interests. Thinking in terms of power relations between classes can help to create an international movement of solidarity to resist the empire. Jung Mo Sung contends that theologians need to critically reflect on economics. This includes critiquing the unlimited desire for wealth and resisting the absolutization of private property. Mario Aguilar's contribution focuses on God who suffers as a victim with the victims, including the victims of African conflicts and the Latin American dictatorships. As the truths of these situations emerge, the perspective of the victims is critical to moving forward. While addressed from a variety of perspectives (African American male, Korean Brazilian male, Latin American, US and European contexts, etc.), there are overlapping themes of the perspective of the marginalized and countering empire, both important in our increasingly globalized world.

2. Liberation theologies in the United States.[5] This section focuses on US-based scholars and activists speaking to our two overarching themes: crossover dialogue—between contexts and disciplines, and reflection on the implications of liberationist discourse for the transformation of theology itself. Rosemary Radford Ruether suggests a theology of letting go. Mediating groups within imperial nations, such as Friends of Sabeel USA, struggle against their own governments to get them to let go of power, in this case to end the oppression of Palestinians. Benjamín Valentín articulates three paths for liberation theology. Socioeconomic and cultural injustice should be merged to address recognition and redistribution together. Bonds should be created and strengthened between these communities of struggle. We need constructive and creative theologies. Tink Tinker's article provides a framework for American Indian liberation theology. It must acknowledge the tensions with Christianity as the religion of the colonizer, use its own history, and reject the imposition of categories like private ownership. Emilie Townes questions the invisibility of color in our orthodoxies. Diversity in all its permutations remains ignored. To counter this, we need to "help create the spaces we know must be there."

Again similar themes emerge. Theologies need to come from the people: rich and poor, white and black, letting go of power, talking about race, and practicing alternatives to the existing hierarchies. Particularities and intersections are both important. This resonates globally too.

3. Liberation theologies around the world. The third section has scholars and activists from outside the United States speaking to the two themes of crossover dialogue and the transformation of theology. Nestor Medina sets ground rules for a Latino/a Canadian theology. One must understand and analyze the dynamics of the reality of Latino/as in Canada. Setting this reality into the larger context of migrants in Canada, its policy of multiculturalism should be interrogated. Heike Walz notes three ways forward for liberation theology. First, it should take into account intercultural perspectives on gender, particularly those of the global South. Second, dialogues must happen between women and men on theology, sex, gender, and sexuality. And finally, there should be a focus on human rights. Mitri Raheb sees the promise of liberation and the illusion of a new era in the Arab Revolutions from a Palestinian perspective. Citing key moments in history as well as aspects of the situation now, he suggests seven components for a public theology of liberation. These include multiparty systems, a solution to the Palestinian question and a prophetic theology to uncover hypocrisy. From the context of India, Wati Longchar asserts indigenous theology's distinctive contribution as "space-centered," focusing on collective justice, recentering theology on the relationship between land, God, and people. Sylvia Marcos highlights the epistemological framework of indigenous theologies, which blend indigenous traditions with Christianity to form an embodied theology with its collective way of understanding God. From contexts as varied as Palestinian liberation, German feminism, and Canadian migration come similar themes of understanding the perspectives of people at the heart of the situation, the importance of intersectionalities, and of land.

4. Practicing liberation theology. While all of our authors practice as well as theologize, this section focuses specifically on practice.[6] Jenny Te Paa's chapter argues that there needs to be transformative attention paid to the educational blueprint underlying all intellectual frameworks. Only when liberation pedagogy is addressed can the teaching of theology be instrumental in transforming material conditions. Ivan Petrella argues that liberation theology needs to expand beyond theology itself. One can work from the standpoint of the oppressed, think about institutions and idolatry in realms outside theology. Seminaries and graduate schools should educate theologians to also be skilled in another field, and there

should be undercover liberation theologians practicing in other fields. We need to be trained to practice and to reflect on that practice. The next section shows some of this developing today.

5. The future of liberation theologies. Here, PhD students' focus on liberation issues help us see some of the future areas of research. Jeremy Kirk's article examines the blockbuster film Avatar through the lens of liberation theology. He analyzes the problems that emerge when liberation tends toward popular messianism and complicity with the powers that be. For Charlene Sinclair, blackness shows how a society has structured power and hegemony, hence, structural transformation is imperative. Placed into dialogue with Karl Marx's critique of political economy, this imperative becomes clearer. William Walker's article considers the drug trade along the US-Mexico border. Using liberation methodology, he articulates the larger context of globalization, the drug war in Mexico, and possible theological and ethical responses. Malik Sales' article looks at resistive performance through the example of Melle Mel's Beat Street Breakdown. Performative events can be liberation theology as a historical project. Again, while the variety of approaches to liberation are clear and new themes such as attention to the arts appear to be emerging, threads flow back to other liberation theologies, black theology, a critique of economic and political policies, and so forth, building on what others have done before them.

With this wide variety of approaches to liberation, this book aims to reach a wider audience of undergraduates and graduates in religious studies and theology to provoke discussion of the future of liberation theologies. As you read this book, think about what speaks to your context and what else might need to be addressed. We invite you to continue the work of liberation.

Reading tips:

Although ordered chronologically according to when the talks were initially presented, these chapters could be approached in several different ways: those addressing economic themes, race, ethnicity; those working inside the United States; those working in developing countries; those working with varied religious traditions; those speaking about liberation theology and its possibilities broadly; those speaking in specific contexts, intersections, interdisciplinarity, male and female perspectives; and scholars of color and white scholar perspectives, age, and so forth. I encourage you to mix and match. For example:

• Empire and Economics: Hopkins, Rieger, Sung, Walker, and Ruether

- Land: Hopkins, Ruether, Tinker, Raheb, Longchar, and Marcos
- Race and Ethnicity: Townes, Medina, Longchar, Marcos, Te Paa, Kirk, and Sinclair
- United States based: Hopkins, Rieger, Ruether, Valentin, Tinker, Townes, Kirk, Sinclair, Walker, and Sales
- Non–United States: Sung, Aguilar, Medina, Walz, Raheb, Longchar, Marcos, Te Paa, and Petrella
- Two-Thirds World: Palestine: Ruether, and Raheb
- Latin America: Sung, Aguilar, Petrella, Walz, Marcos, and Walker
- Specific Contexts: Ruether, Tinker, Townes, Medina, Raheb, Longchar, Marcos, and Te Paa
- Indigenous: Tinker, Longchar, Marcos, and Te Paa

Notes

1. Gutiérrez is a Peruvian priest who has worked in and with base communities for decades.
2. See, for example, Boesak (1976), Boff and Boff (1979), Cone (1988), Gutiérrez (1974), Pieris (1988), and Ruether (1983).
3. See Cox (1988).
4. Even at its beginnings, liberation theology emerged from Protestant communities. It was simply stronger and more prevalent within Catholicism.
5. Ada María Isasi Díaz presented in this group as well and contributed a piece to this work, which sadly we could not include due to her death earlier in 2012. Her presentation articulated four characteristics critical to liberation theologies in the twenty-first century: to be "of" the people, to uphold the option for the poor, to contribute to concrete historical projects, and to denounce oppressive ideological superstructures.
6. Two of our presenters, Avaren Ipsen and Monica Coleman, could not contribute but their work extends the field into the domains of the pastoral, mental health, sex, sexual violence, and the sex trade. See, for example, Avaren Ipsen, 2009, *Sex Working and the Bible,* London: Equinox. And Monica Coleman, 2010, *The Dinah Project: A Handbook for Congregational Response to Sexual Violence,* Eugene: Wipf & Stock.

Bibliography

Boesak, A. 1976. *Farewell to Innocence: A Socio-Ethical Study on Black Theology and Black Power.* Maryknoll: Orbis Books.

Boff, L., and C. Boff. 1979. *Introducing Liberation Theology*, 1. Liberation and Theology. Translated by Paul Burns. Tunbridge Wells: Burns & Oates.

Cone, J. 1988. *Black Theology of Liberation*. Maryknoll: Orbis Books.

Cox, Harvey. 1988. *The Silencing of Leonardo Boff: The Vatican and the Future of World Christianity*. London: Collins.

Gutiérrez, G. 1974. *A Theology of Liberation: History, Politics and Salvation*. Translated by Sister Caridad Inda and John Eagleson. London: SCM.

Pieris, A. 1988. *An Asian Theology of Liberation*. London: Bloomsbury T&T Clark.

Ruether, R. R. 1983. *Sexism and God Talk*. London: SCM.

PART I

Overall State of Liberation Theology

CHAPTER 1

Resisting Imperial Peace: Theological Reflections

Dwight N. Hopkins
dhopkins@uchicago.edu

M y starting point on this topic of "Resisting Imperial Peace: Theological Reflections" is the assumption of the intent of the creation narrative or myth in the book of Genesis. That is to say, that God created humankind in order to share in the beauty of all of creation, especially nature—earth, wind, fire, and water. All that exists in these four realms are God's gift to humankind insofar as human beings recognize that we are stewards of the natural and human ecology belonging to God.

God saw that all of creation, all of the ecology, is good. And this goodness takes its meaning from the fact that something greater than the human capacity and the human will crafted this creation. Because this creation is greater than human capabilities and because this creation originates from an ultimate divinity, creation, all of it, belongs to God. And so, stewardship, in this respect, is the human vocation to accept as a blessing all of creation. In addition, it is to accept the human role of cultivators and nurturers of minerals in the earth, the space of the wind, the water ways of life, and the energy of fire.

If we are blessed by God to assume the awesome and loving responsibility to embrace all dimensions of creation as part of us, since the same God made everything and everything made is both part of God and part of each other, then stewardship suggests an equal participation in all of creation. The first theological principle of divine creative act is a mutual and equal participation in human responsibility. In this sense, to be human is to realize that one's full potential is realized through this equal and shared participation in and with creation.

The question of imperial peace disrupts both the creative act of the divinity and the purpose of being human. The phrase "imperial peace" itself is by definition a contradiction in terms. To be "imperial" is to export a domestic way of being where divine creation is hoarded in private ownership. Stewardship and what it means to be human both become synonymous with privately owning God's creation—specifically the earth, wind, fire, and water. The disruption caused by the "process of the imperial" brings an entire baggage of human centered lifestyles. At the level of political economy, it denotes developing, first, in the domestic realm a rapid redistribution of economic wealth and society's capital upward into smaller numbers of hands. The force of this definition of stewardship and human purpose cuts against the grain of the original narrative of the creation story. Restated, God owns all that God creates, gifts it to all humanity, and this gift provides the possibility for human equal sharing as stewards. To be human is to accept God's ownership, God's offer of stewardship, and God providing the possibility for full maturation of human potential.

Yet the imperial contradicts all of this. Its monopolized private ownership and accumulation of the earth, wind, fire, and water becomes so saturated within the borders of its own country that it is forced to seek international outlets for more accumulation, more privatization, and more monopolization of creation. But this pursuit of a warped and sinful understanding of both stewardship and what it means to be human meets global societies which claim, likewise, to be stewards of the divinity's creation. These countries, also, are stewards of God's creation in their own domestic realms. So the thirst for human accumulation, privatization, and monopolization, on the part of the imperial, inevitably produces violence. On a state to state level, this violence is armed conflict. The armed conflict of war is the most obvious logical extension of the imperial.

There are, however, other forms of imperial extension of its domestic monopolization into the international realm. In today's realities, it is often more effective to be imperial not by the violence of war, the rituals of armed conflict, and occupation of other countries' share in creation. Rather, perhaps a more subtle, sinister, and baffling act of the imperial is the negative globalization of culture. Here the transcendent reach of the global becomes its own god.

Acting as its own god over against God's creative act in Genesis, the imperial tries to create a false peace. It gives the appearance of peace by not producing violent war. Instead it conjures and spreads its own values. It hopes to export transcendent values of the imperial. The imperial hopes that other countries will internalize new values. The point of the religion of globalization is to craft new values to accompany the new person. First is the value of individualism. If the imperial is to succeed as the new god throughout the earth, it has to decouple the idea, particularly in Third World indigenous cultures, that the individual is linked to, defined by, accountable to, and responsible for his or her family and extended family. A sense of communalism and sacrifice of individual gain for the sake of a larger community stands in stark contradiction to the imperial. When an individual converts to the values of the imperial and reorients his or her self-worth and feeling of worthiness to a mode of individual gain, regardless of the well-being of those around him or her, this person has participated in imperial peace. The spread of the value of individualism is a central value for the successful spread of the imperial without the imperial using violent war.

Individualism opens up the additional value of accumulation of things for the individual's primary benefit. In other words, gaining and amassing personal possession as a means of acquiring more personal possessions flows from a focus on the self for the self. This acquisitive desire manifests itself in diverse ways. It downplays sharing. It weakens the art of negotiation and compromise. It blinds a vision of mutuality. And it fosters a utilitarian way of being in the world where people, places, and things become tools for and stepping-stones toward increased personal profit. On the political level, such a value breeds a type of "monopoly capitalist democracy" constituted by subordination of the many for the few. This form of democracy employs the many to attain more resources for the few. As a political value, such a democracy equates the common good and the larger civic welfare with pragmatic results for the elite. In the economic sphere, it is an internal feeling that prompts the individual to pursue profit to gain more personal profit. It privileges the importance of commodities and material goods. Economic wealth is valued as one of the highest virtues in the definition of the new human being. Akin to an addiction (when left to mature), it motivates, gnaws at, and compels the new converted person to make life-and-death decisions based on the amount of wealth he or she has. The ownership of wealth commodities and/or the hunger for this ownership controls the person's perception of the worth of life and death.

A return to our initial discussion about a theology of creation helps us to figure out how to resist this imperial peace by advancing an alternative theological vision. Actually, it is a recasting of the initial creation story of Genesis. God created all there is and all there is belongs to God for human beings to share equally.

Kim Yong-Bock (Korean) adds another theological dimension to a theology of creation. Yong-Bock approaches the subject matter with the theme of covenant between God and the poor. More specifically, the new covenant appears in the divine spiritual revelation in Jesus and his relation to those lacking material resources for a wholesome life. Yong-Bock explains:

> The most dramatic expression of the socio-economic dimension of the new covenant is found in the early church, especially in Acts 2:42–47 and 4:32–5:11. This is the protection of the community of the faithful, who are the new people of God: "The faithful lived together and owned everything in common; they sold their goods and possessions and shared out the proceeds among themselves according to what each needed." "None of their members was ever in want." That is, there were no poor. (1991, 80)

Young-Bock goes on to infer how in today's human family, established on the monopolization of private ownership of wealth and resources for a small sector of society, the cited book of Acts passages are dismissed as utopian or eschatological or hyperbole. That is, Christians and other readers of the Bible utilize a hermeneutics of me-first to misinterpret the community, communal values, and common good accent of this sacred history. Quite the contrary, asserts Yong-Bock, the early church provided a radical paradigm in the hierarchical and exploitative context of the slavery political economy in the Roman empire. Original Christian communities challenged the overall political and economic make up in the accepted social normalcy. Consequently, due to a revolutionary hope offered by Christianity, freed persons and slaves joined the counter-status quo Jesus movement. Thus, the "way" for the poor became a communal calling.

And, from a closer reading of Acts, sacred political economy yielded collective benefits for all members of the community when one prioritized the poor. The group of believers united in their hearts and souls without monopolizing possessions because all materialities were held in common. This social arrangement left no one wanting; each received according to her or his condition. Moreover, the epistle of James 2:1–9 amplifies the clarification of the early church: "My brothers [and sisters], do not try to combine faith in Jesus Christ, our glorified Lord, with the making of distinctions between classes of people. . . . It is those who are poor according to the world that God chose, to be rich in faith and to be heirs of the kingdom which [God] promised to those who love [God]." Prior to Roman emperor Constantine co-opting Christianity to serve the wealthy of the empire, the early church lived with a faith that opted on the side of the majority of the people, the poor, the enslaved, the working sectors, the marginalized, and those generally without material hope: those "economically destitute—because of their loss of property or their lack of inheritance, or because of their having been robbed by the powerful and rich" (Yong-Bock 1991, 81–2).[1]

In such a way, the early church's economic and political configurations provided interactions starting with the poor, the majority, and, through them, the rest of the society, including the wealthy. The primordial gathering of believers, thereby, was able to experience the new social benefits of equal ownership and proportional advantage to all. The political economy for the poor, Yong-Bock concludes, permeated the primal Christian community and the biblical text. Because the God-human covenant as the content of theological anthropology defended the poor via covenant codes, legal statutes, and the prophets in the Hebrew Scriptures (so-called Old Testament) and by Jesus's mission and covenant in the Christian Scriptures (so-called New Testament), the poor became the protagonists in biblical history and become the criteria for faithful Christian (and, one could imagine, humanist[2]) witness today.

Theologically, we therefore can reason, the first organized Christian communities and the Bible view God in a definitive political economy manner. God stands as the ultimate creator, owner, and giver of all wealth and resources found on, beneath, and above the earth. The question of the earth, wind, water, fire, and the components of technologies derive from the grace or granting of the divine. In broader strokes, the entire creation and ingredients currently harnessed by woman and man find their origin before the arrival of human communities and appear as a consequence of some power greater than human capabilities. Creation just is. And we partake of and benefit from it.

Imperial peace is a deceptive peace. It can spread internationally without the presence of violent war, at least for a period of time. It gives the appearance of peace while it extends its imperial tentacles through imperial values that are just as effective as outright violent war. So in this respect, this imperial peace produces the same results as violent war. The phrase "imperial peace" is a contradiction in terms. Most fundamentally it contradicts the God of creation of mutual sharing, collective stewardship, and realization of the full human potential.

Notes

1. Yong-Bock supplies additional biblical passages as data: Micah 2:2–5; Deuteronomy 10:17–18, 14–15, 16:19; Psalm 82:3; Exodus 23:3; Samuel 22:28; Isaiah 1:21–23, 25:4, 61:1; Amos 2:6, 4:1; Leviticus 19 and 23; Hosea 12:8–9; Luke 1:53, 4:18ff, 5:29–32, 6:5, 20, 21, 24, 25, 14:15–24, 16:19ff, 18:18ff, 21:1ff; and Matthew 22:1–1, 26:31–46. Also see Engelbert Mveng (1994, 163) for further biblical warrants for a communal political economy.

   As we employ biblical pointers, we are aware of shortcomings even in the text itself. For instance, one has to be careful how the exodus theme is used. Robert Allen Warrior cautions against such a theme because there existed indigenous people already in Canaan who were violently conquered by the Hebrew people exiting from slavery in Egypt. And Renita Weems decries the pornographic domestic violence language that some of the biblical prophets deployed as tropes.

2. Kwame Wiredu (1992, 194), Kwame Gyekye (1987, 19–20, 154), and N. K. Dzobo (1992, 226–27) argue for a form of humanism which I take to imply an obligation to the poor's well-being.

Bibliography

Dzobo, N. K. 1992. "Values in a Changing Society: Man, Ancestors and God." In *Person in Community*, ed. Kwasi Wiredu and Kwame Gyekye, 223–42. Washington: The Council for Research in Values and Philosophy.

Gyekye, K. 1987. *An Essay on African Philosophical Thought: The Akan Conceptual Scheme*. Cambridge: Cambridge University Press.

Mveng, E. 1994. "Impoverishment and Liberation: A Theological Approach for Africa and the Third World." In *Paths of African Theology*, ed. Rosino Gibellini, 154–65. Maryknoll: Orbis Books.

Warrior, R. A. 1991. "A Native American Perspective: Canaanites, Cowboys, and Indians." In *Voices from the Margins: Interpreting the Bible in the Third World*, ed. R. S. Sugirtharajah, 287–95. Maryknoll: Orbis Books.

Weems, R. 1995. *Battered Love: Marriage, Sex, and Violence in the Hebrew Prophets*. Minneapolis: Fortress.

Wiredu, K. 1992. "Moral Foundations of an African Culture." In *Person in Community*, ed. Kwasi Wiredu and Kwame Gyekye, 193–206. Washington: The Council for Research in Values and Philosophy.

Yong-Bock, K. 1991. "Covenant with the Poor: Toward a New Concept of Economic Justice". In *Healing for God's World: Remedies from Three Continents*, ed. Kofi Asare Opoku, Kim Yong-Bock, and Antoinette Clark Wire, 61–111. New York: Friendship.

CHAPTER 2

Context Is What Hurts: Rethinking Contextual Theology in Light of Empire and Economics

Joerg Rieger
jrieger@smu.edu

Contextual Theology Revisited through the Lens of Empire

A little over a decade ago, in 1996, at a session at the American Academy of Religion in memory of Frederick Herzog, who was one of the few white liberation theologians in the United States,[1] I raised some questions about the usefulness of contextual theology as it is often understood and practiced. The problem with a certain kind of contextual theology is that it tends to take context at face value, without reading between the lines. In classical, nineteenth-century liberal theology, for instance, the context of humanity was assumed to be universal. Paul Tillich still assumed the context of humanity to be universal, shaped by the experience of meaninglessness, anxiety, and despair.

In recent decades, context has been defined in terms of particular settings, which are, however, often still taken at face value. Tom Driver (1977) once talked about "doing theology in a warm bathtub," which some might consider to be the context of white middle-class theologians. When the contexts of women and minorities are taken at face value in this manner, the result is that contextual theology is understood as special interest theology, dealing with particular contexts and interests that are relevant to some groups but not to others.

Understanding context not as what appears to be closest to home but as that which hurts can help us address this problem of contextual theology.[2] The pain that women in a patriarchal society experience, for instance, ties together women and men. The pain to which African Americans in a racist society are exposed ties together black and white. The pain inflicted on working-class people under the conditions of late capitalism ties together workers and bosses. These contexts are not a matter of special interest because they link together those who experience pain and those who are somehow involved in inflicting it and who are thus also affected by it. Context as that which hurts may not be immediately visible from the positions involved in inflicting pain, but when the connections are pointed out, new perspectives open up that can lead to transformation.

The approach that I am suggesting here has deep theological roots. Context as that which hurts points to a common pain that is expressed by the apostle Paul's reflections on the church as the body of Christ: "If one member suffers, all suffer together with it" (1 Cor 12:26). The body, Paul notes, cannot survive without attention to its common pain or without attention to what is often considered the "inferior members": "The eye cannot say to the hand hands, 'I have not need of you,' nor again the head to the feet, 'I have no need of you'" (1 Cor 12:21). As the labor unions put it: "An injury to one is an injury to all." This insight leads to a fundamental reversal: the common interest is not located at the top or in universals that do not exist (like "humanity in general" or even "women in general"). The common interest is located in situations of pain and struggle that tie us together.

Today, we are pulled ever closer together in our common pain by the forces of empire and globalization, across all the established boundaries of region, nation, culture, creed, race, gender, and class. The forces of empire and globalization should not be understood as merely political or economic, as their reach goes far beyond politics and economics. Empire can be understood as "massive concentrations of power which permeate all aspects of life and which cannot be controlled by any one actor alone" (Rieger 2009, 2). The forces of empire combine dominant economic, political, cultural, religious, intellectual, and emotional powers in order to shape the world and its inhabitants to the core. The context that needs to be addressed by contextual theology is, therefore, the context of empire. This is where the common pain is rooted, which destroys not only the lives of the victims of empire but also the lives of the victimizers, who damage their own humanity by disregarding the humanity of others.

When we talk about empire in the current context, it is important to note that the most visible manifestations of empire, like warfare and direct violence, are only the tip of the iceberg. The hard power of bombs, guns, beatings, rape, and even the hard power of forced structural adjustment programs needs to be seen in conjunction with the soft power of diplomacy, cultural projects, trade, loans, and well-meaning development programs. As empire takes postcolonial forms, it is able to integrate postmodern pluralism, multiculturalism, and even certain democratic ways of life. In these new forms, economics plays an ever greater role.[3]

The common pain that defines our context must, therefore, be considered in structural terms. This does not mean that personal experiences of pain and the many different shapes that such experiences can take should be disregarded; personal experiences of pain help us broaden and deepen our understanding of the structures. It is simply a reminder that we need to dig deeper in terms of what contributes to the creation of these experiences, and that we need to develop broader horizons in terms of the collective shape that these experiences take.

In discussing the structural nature of our common pain, new tools have proven to be very useful, in particular postcolonial theory and subaltern studies. These approaches have helped us look at a broader range of pain in our current context. The subaltern studies groups in India and Latin America, for instance, have introduced an awareness for the pain generated along the lines of gender, caste, age, social status, and other factors often overlooked. Postcolonial theory has contributed an understanding of the complexity of this pain, as it shapes up in hybrid contexts, where many different factors interact and no clear lines can be drawn. In this regard, postcolonial theory has also helped us to gain a new sense for the predicament of the colonizers, who are also affected by hybridity and whose identity is, therefore, pulled deeper into this common pain than we had ever imagined.

These efforts at grasping the complexity of our common pain are crucial to the future of contextual theology, as they also emphasize the need for detailed historical study of particular contexts. Nevertheless, the problem in the United States is that we have never really addressed one of the key factors of our common pain that was presupposed by the subaltern studies groups and many postcolonial approaches, namely the notion of class. In the United States, we are only gradually discovering the importance of the notion of class and its intersection with other forms of oppression. Even the critique of empire that is developing in the United States often overlooks class issues and moves straight to a critique of racism or ethnocentrism.

Economics and Class Analysis

If empire takes an economic shape in our time, we need to discuss the topic of class once again. At the 1996 event in memory of Herzog, almost all panelists talked about the importance of economics for the future of liberation theology, without prior agreement that we would focus on this topic. Susan Thistlethwaite's (1998, 21) perceptive analysis still rings true that a major roadblock for liberation theology in the United States is the failure of economic analysis to take hold.

Of course, investigating class does not imply a disregard for other factors such as gender and race. In the United States, bell hooks and Angela Davis, two prominent African American women thinkers have reminded us of the interplay of all of these factors. African American womanist theology has likewise upheld the intersection of gender, race, and class, although in theological discourse the notion of class remains under-analyzed and under-theorized.

When class has been mentioned by theologians in the United States, it has been mostly in order to recognize the situation of the poor and less fortunate members of our societies. What is mostly absent is an understanding of class in terms of the relationship between the various classes. Sociological models of stratification have added to this one-dimensional way of thinking about class. The discussion of income stratification, for instance, often focuses on lateral descriptions of various levels at the expense of addressing the relation between the classes.

A first step toward a more adequate analysis of class is understanding class not in terms of income levels but in terms of power. Economist Michael Zweig (2012, 36), for instance, has suggested that we consider the power that people have at work. According to this model, 63 percent of all Americans can be considered working class, while 35 percent belong to the middle class and only 2 percent to the ruling class.[4] The working class, according to Zweig, which includes large numbers of white-collar workers, is defined by the fact that it has very little power over its work, as others determine what needs to be done and give the orders. When seen in this light, many traditional middle-class occupations are moving closer to the working class as well. While university professors, for instance, tend to understand themselves as members of the professions with some power, their status is not what it once was. Not only is tenure under attack, the latest push for so-called outcomes evaluations in the classroom implies yet another effort to control the work of professors more tightly.

The question is how we portray the common interest that emerges here. How do we help people get in touch with context as that which hurts? Liberation theology is particularly relevant in regard to this question as the Jewish and Christian traditions have plenty of resources. Jesus's reiteration of the double commandment, to love God and to love one's neighbor as oneself (Mark 12:30–31), might be interpreted not only as a reminder that our neighbors are not alien to us but also that they are not merely objects of charity or social service. Jesus's statement hints at a connection of neighbor and self, and so our neighbors need to be understood as part of who we are. Unfortunately, people often fail to recognize this relationship, a mistake that helps prop up the system, as it allows the old strategies of divide and conquer.

In this context, we need to note that class warfare is alive and well. In the United States, decades of chipping away at salaries and benefits as well as organized labor have created rising inequality, and there seems to be no end in sight. The so-called jobless recovery of the economy after the recession of 2008 and 2009 is no accident or natural catastrophe but the result of cutting jobs and benefits, and of the outsourcing of work. Internationally, neoliberal globalization has developed ever more effective ways of securing the power of transnational corporations and their investors, for instance through so-called free trade agreements that tend to favor power and wealth.

Since class warfare is covered up extremely well in the United States, many people's discontent finds other ways to express itself. As a result, anger is channeled in the wrong directions, toward ethnic and racial minorities, away from that which imposes pressure on everyday people, like the job, the boss, the economy, and conservative politics. Liberals are not off the hook on this issue; they have developed similar blind spots when it comes to the reality of the class struggle that is waged from the top down.

The topic of class struggle is better addressed and understood elsewhere. During a visit to Argentina in 2007, I watched a public TV program on the failures of globalization and privatization. What was most instructive was that this program not only described the class struggle waged against working people but also presented alternatives rooted in initiatives of workers to self-organize and take over abandoned factories. These initiatives were so successful that eventually the bosses, who had abandoned the factories, returned in order to claim what they considered their property.[5]

In recent developments in the United States, the Occupy Wall Street movement has helped create some awareness of the tensions and opportunities of class, by distinguishing between the 1 percent and the 99 percent. In this context, a liberation theology of the future will need to address not only what is happening to those who no longer benefit from the system but also to those who are gaining enormous wealth and power as others are suffering.

No doubt, a deeper awareness of the realities of class is crucial not only to an understanding of how life shapes up under the conditions of neoliberal capitalism but also to the question of how we imagine God in the midst of these tensions. Moreover, the awareness of class can help clarify some important issues that are often overlooked when people deal with the categories of gender, sexuality, race, or ethnicity to the exclusion of class.

First, understanding class reminds us that our identities are always constructs. There is nothing natural about class, as people do not belong to the working class or the ruling class by nature. As a result, there can be no identity politics in terms of class, where identity is considered a given, to be taken at face value. This matches contemporary positions in the study of race, ethnicity, gender, and sexuality, which have argued that these categories are also constructed rather than natural. The notion of class can help us deepen these positions, especially if we understand that class differences are not something to be celebrated, which leads to the second point.

An understanding of class reminds us that an appreciation of otherness and difference is not sufficient and can even become problematic. It would be ludicrous to celebrate the difference of classes or to seek their reconciliation in terms of a "unity in difference." Class differences need to be challenged when they take exploitative forms and when they lead to the domination of one class over the other. This has implications for how we deal with remedial projects like affirmative action: while it is important to counter the results of systemic racism and sexism in our society, merely integrating people back into the system does not address the deeper problems. The system itself will need to be challenged.

Finally, let me reiterate that class reminds us of the fact that binaries are not as irrelevant as the postmodern academy has made them appear. There is a difference between those who own the means of production (or those who have control over them, such as major shareholders or CEOs) and those who do not. This difference is not simply a matter of money; more importantly, it is a matter of power. In this context, those in the middle, the members of the so-called middle class, are not off the hook but are torn between the ruling class and the working class, leaning for the most part in one or the other direction, without ever having the benefits or the security of the ruling class.

An International Movement of Solidarity

The biggest challenge for a liberation theology of the future is how to build international movements of solidarity. Class issues are especially critical in this regard, as they are international by design, due to the global spread of neoliberal capitalism. The fate of workers in the United States, whether they realize it or not, is much more intimately connected to workers in other countries than to the ruling class in the United States. Race and ethnicity have often been used in top-down forms of class struggle to cover up precisely this fact, so that white workers are led to identify more with their white bosses than with their African American, Latino, or Asian coworkers. While it sounds paradoxical, working people are also connected by the fact that they are played off against each other as well as against the unemployed by their employers.

To be sure, issues of gender, race, ethnicity, and sexuality also transcend borders and demand international movements of solidarity. Yet race and ethnicity have different histories in different contexts, and even gender dynamics are not as universal as it may appear. This is why Muslim feminists, for instance, have often had to remind Western women that their struggles shape up differently and that what appears oppressive to one group may be a tool of liberation for others.[6] As a result, even international solidarity in terms of gender, race, ethnicity, and sexuality can benefit from international solidarity established on the basis of class.

A new understanding of class will also help us deepen what we currently understand as solidarity. Progressives in the so-called First World have often understood solidarity as a decision of the will to support others who are less fortunate. This mindset has made positive contributions to many important projects, including fair trade, international aid, and advocacy for human rights. At the same time, this kind of solidarity has also led to a certain patronizing attitude, especially when things went well, and to burnout, especially when they did not.

The next step would be to consider what I am calling deep solidarity. Deep solidarity is based on a sense that we are all in the same boat, that there is something that ties us together despite all our differences that must not be overlooked. Despite of significant differences in terms of economics, race, ethnicity, sexuality, and gender, there is something that ties together what the Occupy Movement has called the 99 percent, namely the fact that most of us are no longer benefiting from the structures of late capitalism. In the United States, this fact was covered up for a long time by the availability of credit at all levels, from credit cards to reverse mortgages. Now that credit is no longer as easily available and as much of people's net worth has disappeared in the housing and unemployment crisis, we are becoming clearer about our actual location within the system. Economists have talked about the "Judas Economy," pointing out that while being located in the First World has often been beneficial for workers, this is less and less the case.[7]

In the United States in particular, the development of deep solidarity is actively opposed by various mechanisms. Race in particular has been often used to divide those who would be natural allies in terms of class and even in terms of gender and sexuality. The ruling class has maintained its power by playing off white workers against black workers. And even some well-meaning efforts at overcoming racism and sexism have unwittingly contributed to the weakening of deep solidarity. When working-class white men are made to feel that they are the main perpetrators of oppression along the lines of race and gender, for instance, they often get the false impression that they have no other option but to align themselves with white men of the ruling class, who actively compete for the support of the white working class.

If, however, working-class white men were to understand that the small advantages that they enjoy in terms of their race and gender positions are used by the system to play them off against racial minorities and women, deep solidarity would become an option. After all, white male workers have significantly more in common with black workers, female workers, and, even, immigrant workers than with their white bosses. While the trade unions have not always fought these challenges effectively, they have learned a great deal in recent years. One example is the growing union support for immigrant labor.

In these contexts, many of our religious traditions can help us imagine and reimagine deep solidarity. At the heart of worship in Israel is the Exodus, that is, a liberation movement in which God took clear sides. Furthermore, the support for widows, orphans, and strangers in the Hebrew Bible is often argued on the grounds that Israel itself knows what it is to be a stranger. Jesus's message of good news to the poor presupposes an understanding of solidarity, which includes the possibility that people put themselves on the side of the poor.

Conclusions

One of the common criticisms of liberation movements is that their efforts invariably result in simple reversals. It is assumed that the working class, for instance, merely wants to take the place of the ruling class and continue with business as usual. Yet such reversals are hard to imagine for various reasons.

If context is that what hurts, there can be no easy homogenization of contexts into a dominant context. If we take seriously the pain endured by various sorts of oppression, no straightforward top-down response is possible. And even if this common pain were only the pain of the working class, the 60 percent of all Americans who are working class cannot be transposed into the ruling class as it exists at present, where 400 individuals have more wealth than 60 percent of all Americans.[8]

It would be naïve, of course, to assume that sin is only a matter of the one-percent ruling class and that the ninety-nine percent are without sin. Yet the sins of the people are different than the sins of the rulers. Where the sin of the rulers can be described by Augustine's classic notion of pride, where human beings put themselves in the place of God, the sins of the people might be described as false humility, that is, not taking their own powers seriously enough.

The problem of liberation movements is, therefore, not that they produce simple reversals. The weak points and distortions of liberation movements will have to be investigated as they take shape, but the fact that such weak points exist should not prevent us from continuing to envision a different world where suffering is reduced and life-and-death struggles are less common than they are now. In this regard, a liberation theology of the future agrees with the motto of the World Forums of Liberation: another world is possible.

Notes

1. The presentations were published in Rieger (1998b).
2. See Rieger (1998a).
3. Michael Hardt and Antonio Negri (2000) define empire in contradistinction to an older imperialism, having to do to a large degree with the movements of transnational capital. In discussion with Hardt and Negri, Ellen Meiksins Wood (2003) makes a valid argument regarding the ongoing importance of the nation state in shoring up and supporting the power of transnational late capitalism.
4. In the first edition of this book, published in 2000 (pp. 34–35), the working class was at 62 percent, the middle class at 36 percent, and the ruling class at 2 percent.
5. See also Lewis and Klein (2005).
6. The role of the veil is one example. See Yegenoglu (2002).

7. See Wolman and Colamosca (1997).

8. These numbers have been verified by PolitiFact, http://www.politifact. com/wisconsin/statements/2011/mar/10/michael-moore/michael-moore-says-400-americans-have-more-wealth-/, accessed February 27, 2012.

Bibliography

Driver, T. 1977. *Patterns of Grace: Human Experience as Word of God.* San Francisco: Harper and Row, 1–28.

Hardt, M., and A. Negri. 2000. *Empire.* Cambridge: Harvard.

Lewis, A., and N. Klein. 2005. *The Take, a Documentary Film.* www.thetake.org, accessed February 27, 2012.

Rieger, J., ed. 1998a. "Developing a Common Interest Theology from the Underside." In *Liberating the Future: God, Mammon and Theology, ed. Joerg Rieger,* 124–41. Minneapolis: Fortress.

———. 1998b. *Liberating the Future: God, Mammon, and Theology.* Minneapolis: Fortress.

———. 2009. *Christ and Empire: From Paul to Postcolonial Times.* Minneapolis: Fortress.

Thistlethwaite, S. B. 1998. "On Becoming a Traitor: The Academic Liberation Theologian and the Future." In *Liberating the Future: God, Mammon and Theology,* ed. Joerg Rieger, 14–26. Minneapolis: Fortress.

Wolman, W., and A. Colamosca. 1997. *The Judas Economy: The Triumph of Capital and the Betrayal of Work.* Reading: Addison-Wesley.

Wood, E. M. 2003. *Empire of Capital.* London: Verso.

Yegenoglu, M. 2002. "Sartorial Fabric-ations: Enlightenment and Western Feminism." In *Postcolonialism, Feminism, and Religious Discourse,* ed. Laura Donaldson and Kwok Pui Lan, 82–99. New York: Routledge.

Zweig, M. 2012. *The Working Class Majority: America's Best Kept Secret,* second edition. Ithaca: Cornell University Press.

CHAPTER 3

Theology, Spirit, and the Imperial Economic System

Jung Mo Sung

jungmosung@uol.com.br

There was a time in the history of human thought that theologians used to reflect on the operational aspects of the economy. Today, few theologians construct economic theory or propose economic policy. The economy has been emancipated from the dominion of theology.

But theology has something to say to the economy precisely because this field is fundamental to human life and social relations. Since economic theory and practice are rooted in anthropological, ethical, and, even, theological assumptions, theology must help to unpack and critique these assumptions. Social and economic systems are possessed by a "spirit" that animates them, motivating individuals and groups to consolidate and reproduce the dominant system. Max Weber, for example, said: "The question of the motivating forces in the expansion of modern capitalism is not in the first instance a question of the origin of the capital sums which were available for capitalistic uses, but, above all, of the development of the spirit of capitalism" (1958, 68). Georg Lukács, in his famous book *History and Class Consciousness*, also notes that, in its essence, the power that moves every society is a spiritual power.

It is on this level of the anthropological and theological presuppositions of economic theories and systems and of the spirit that moves society that theological reflections must place their focus. The specific contributions of theology occur in the critical reflection on these aspects, a task that the modern social sciences do not take very seriously and for which they are not well suited. We must dialogue with other sciences, but we must not lose sight of the specificity of theology. We must not transform theology into a secondary economics and sociology. Among several challenges facing theology in this field, I will mention only two. The first is to critique the spirit that moves capitalism. In capitalism, the unlimited desire for wealth is transformed into a fundamental virtue in social life. Premodern societies sought to limit this desire (see, for example, "You shall not covet your neighbor's house" (Exodus 20:17)), but capitalist societies find in the never-ending search for more riches the essential spirit of society and the path by which people are made fully human. The more individuals earn and the more ostentatiously they consume, society considers them to have, and they feel themselves to have, greater value as persons.

In the dominant capitalist culture, consumption has become the measure of a life well-lived, of happiness and of one's essential value as a human being. Thus, the desire to possess what another desires and more than others has come to be considered both a right and a duty. Society no longer proposes appropriate limits for consumption but rather becomes the arena in which one pursues unlimited consumption. In this culture of consumption, mimetic desire and rivalry have become the fundamental reference points in the relations between persons-consumers. This is the spirituality of consumption. The other side of this coin is that the poor, as failed consumers, are considered to be sinners, subhumans, beings lacking the fullness of human dignity. They are considered as "demons" that must be cast out of society.

This logic offers no way to distinguish between property whose function is to assure or sustain the dignity of human life and property that serves to accumulate more property and capital. Indeed, human dignity becomes identified with one's capacity to accumulate more property and to consume more. All of human existence becomes a process of ever-increasing accumulation and consumption.

With the disappearance of this fundamental distinction, we also witness the inversion of the relationship between human rights and property rights. Such essential human rights as the rights to life, work, health, liberty, and citizenship are no longer considered to have priority over the market but rather to be the product of participating in the market. That is, individuals are considered to be humans, bearers of human rights, by virtue of their participation in the market. Property and market become the foundation for human rights.

This leads us to the second problem: the absolutization of private property and of the laws of the capitalist market. The market and private property—two sides of the same coin according to capitalism—are considered to be absolute values that are beyond questioning, the root values by which everything is measured and prioritized. This is the most important idolatry of our time, which demands sacrifices of human dignities and lives. The spirit of this idolatrous imperial system is seducing people all over the world and empowering the current economic globalization.

A theological critique of this absolutization must not fall into the error of applying similar logic and completely denying the value of private property and of the market and of proposing solidarity as the unique principle of an economic system. This tendency to employ "metaphysical" critiques—to deny absolutely—is quite common in ethical and religious discourse. After all, theologians claim to speak in the name of divine and to propose divine projects. Human history, however, clearly teaches us that we can never escape the ambiguity and contradictions that characterize the human condition.

Another difficulty with the critiques offered by religious traditions is that most of these traditions were born and elaborated their ethical principles in premodern contexts, when far simpler economic models were in play. In societies with complex economies such as ours, it is no longer possible to organize the production and distribution of economic goods without the market and forms of private property. The challenge is to hold socially defined goals, such as social justice, in tension with the mechanisms of the market.

To further this discussion, I propose a brief reflection on the economic model of the Jerusalem Community in earliest Christianity. The model presented in the book of Acts cannot be understood as an alternative to the Roman Empire economic system, because it presupposes the existence of a larger community and economic system, based on buying and selling, where they could sell properties and buy goods needed for distribution to the families of their community who were in need.

I am not arguing that the Christian community in Jerusalem had nothing to say to the economic system of their time. I just want to show that critiques and alternative models are not as simple as they might seem. In the case of Acts, what motivated people to sell all they had and hold all property in common was their faith in the resurrection of Jesus and their firm conviction that the end times were at hand. The idea of property as a source of life for the poor and of holding all in common is a radical sign of life and a foreshadowing of eschatological plenitude. This foreshadowing critiques the absolutist character of the all empires and opens perspectives for other possible world and social systems.

The Jerusalem community's model must be understood as an expression of the tension they experienced as they sought to live out a prophetic witness in their particular social environment. Their actions should be understood as God's judgment on the economic model of that time and not as an ideal social project.

The author of Acts makes clear that the social and economic model of that community was not sustainable over time. Luke narrates how Ananias and Sapphira commit fraud (5:2), demonstrating the ambiguity present in this community. While the community remains small, problems can be resolved through a meeting of all the members. But as the community grows, the problem of administration arises (6:16). Widows of Jewish heritage receive preferential treatment, and Greek widows suffer discrimination in the distribution of goods. Eventually a structural problem results: the community experiences hunger. The generations of new resources were insufficient to meet the needs of all members of the community.

This experience presents three types of problems: personal, administrative, and structural. All three need to be considered in any alternative proposals, be it for institutions or for the society as a whole.

The problems confronted by the Jerusalem community in no way invalidate the judgment pronounced by God on the imperial systems. More important for us is the desire of the Jerusalem community to explore alternative social and economic models as an expression of their faith in the resurrection of Jesus. This intimate relationship between faith in the resurrection of the crucified Jesus and the struggle for creating alternative social and economic systems is one of the key subjects for liberation theology.

Bibliography

Lukács, G. 1971. *History and Class Consciousness*. Translated by R. Livingstone. London: Merlin.

Sung, Jung Mo. 2007. *Desire, Market and Religion*. London: SCM.

———. 2011. *The Subject, Capitalism, and Religion: Horizons of Hope in Complex Societies*. New York: Palgrave MacMillan.

Weber, M. 1958. *The Protestant Ethic and the Spirit of Capitalism*. New York: Scribner's.

CHAPTER 4

The Hermeneutics of Bones: Liberation Theology for the Twenty-First Century

Mario I. Aguilar
mia2@st-and.ac.uk

Theological Genesis

The advent of Vatican II (1962–1965) and the Medellín conference of bishops in Latin America (1968) created the possibilities for a Christian reflection on poverty in Latin America.[1] Not only was poverty assumed as a reality but also it was accepted that such reality affected the actions and thoughts of the church. The materially poor entered the church's reflection not solely to request rights and human dignity but their reality challenged the very life of the church, which for all purposes appeared materially rich and powerful. Pastoral agents and clergy started a change in their lifestyle assuming that if they were closer to the poor they would be indeed be closer to Christ (Gutiérrez 1993, 250).

In that climate the so-called theology of liberation developed as a Christian commitment in history, as "a new way to do theology" (Gutiérrez 1985, 15). It challenged a theology done from an armchair and from a position of political power, identified by Gustavo Gutiérrez (1985, 53) as "Christendom" not as "a mental construct" but as a centralized existence in which any other historical existence does not have "an authentic existence." It is important to remember these theological foundations and praxis in any theological reflection concerning liberation theology in the twenty-first century.

Due to the change in the historical project by Latin American theologians they re-elaborated their analyses of events in Latin America that from the 1960s to the 1990s were dominated by the military regimes, their sociopolitical oppression, and their human rights violations.[2] Most of the theological writings that followed a Christian praxis during those three decades related to a general challenge of unjust structures of poverty by Christian communities within Latin America.

However, already by the 1980s the Latin American theologians started cooperating with theologians in Africa and Asia and the single-theological agenda of the poor in history became a larger agenda symbolized by the theme of the Basic Christian Communities and their agency. Through these international meetings it was possible to introduce diversity, change, and challenges to Gutiérrez' agenda, and liberation from sin and injustice within society became complemented by a theological agenda of the option for the poor, a theme to which other Christians in other continents could relate to.[3] Further, challenges to injustice in society became complemented by the challenges of liberation within the churches as well, including theological reflections by women, Hispanics, blacks, and indigenous populations of Latin America and beyond.

Liberating Bones

I have suggested somewhere else that the complexity of liberation theology can only be assumed through a "problem of generations" in which a complex development took place in the social historical contexts as praxis and a theological reflection on praxis and history.[4] Within those complexities, usually misunderstood, has been the commitment to find the image and work of a liberating God within the history, social and political, of the poor and the marginalized. This history of the poor, marginalized, and persecuted has been deeply felt by those who through the political persecution of opponents by the military regimes in Latin America or the killing of thousands in African conflicts such as the Rwandan genocide have had to search for their relatives and loved ones.[5] Thus, one of the ongoing historical realities of injustice that unites the past 40 years of praxis and theology has been the issue of the disappeared and the unaccounted-for bodies and bones of those who were arrested, tortured, and killed by state agents within the various military regimes of the Latin American southern cone.[6]

If liberation theologians have dealt with reflections on praxis, and theology has been considered a "second step," then theological reflections on the aftermath of oppression have not been forthcoming. In continents such as Africa and Latin America where death and the dead are quite prominent, theological narratives have not properly explored the boundaries of a liberation that extends to those killed and their families, to those killed whose bodies were never found, and to those arrested, presumed killed but still "un-dead."

Thirty years after the height of the period of the military regimes in the southern cone of Latin America the English-speaking newspapers still report news about the disappeared, those who were imprisoned and tortured, and the government leaders who are still being tried, convicted, and imprisoned in the twenty-first century.[7] *The Times* of London, for example, reported the burial of the ashes of a mother of the Plaza de Mayo in Argentina, Azucena Villaflor (30 years on, 2005). Mrs. Villaflor had a son of age 17 arrested and made to disappear by the Argentinean authorities in 1977. Her means of protest was to walk around the square every Thursday and to continue alerting the media about the human rights abuses in Argentina. One day she was arrested, tortured, and her body made to disappear. During 2005 the human remains in an unmarked grave were identified as hers. Her daughter, Cecilia, together with some surviving mothers of the disappeared buried her ashes at the Buenos Aires' square opposite the presidential palace. Those mothers of the disappeared, much older 30 years later were still determined to find out what happened to their loved ones. Cecilia's words expressed the whole human story of any forced disappearance when she spoke publicly saying, "I'm never going to be able to tell you how much I love you, Mama, how much I miss you, how much I have needed you over these twenty eight years."

Bones speak very clearly of history; they are like maps of past events. While forensic science helps us to understand what happened to an individual, hermeneutics help us to understand bones as historical texts, and liberation theology provides a reflection on social processes in which the God of life was ignored. For God, the liberating God, was present in those events but witnessed the horrors of the negation of life and the negation of God in society.

One of the greatest possibilities of liberation theology has always been the possibility of utopia, the possibility of dreaming that a better world can eventually come because "utopias are not illusions" but "they are imaginative and creative, but realistic possibilities for the future" (Wilfred 2007, 159). The dreamer is not imagining an outside reality. Instead, through a liberating praxis, through actions that speak of liberation here and now, the dreamer prepares a community for the realities to come, enjoying the immediacy of the Eros, of the desire for God and other human beings, rather than the desire for commodities or for material things. In this, liberation theology connects the utopian dream, and as a result the dreamer, with a historical project.[8]

In the case of genocide, the historical realities of suffering and dehumanization speak at all times of a lack of freedom and of a need for liberation. However, neither those who have suffered nor those who are still suffering are able to see another reality without the possibility of dreaming. Dreaming does not stop during genocide, and utopian moments maintain the sufferer and the victim connected to a world outside the body in a needy sense of touch, of feeling, and of simplicity. For example, during General Pinochet's attempt at the extermination of political opponents—particularly those who were actively opposing his dictatorial regime with arms—torture, violence, degrading treatments, and periods of torture were aimed at destroying the person, destroying hope, and destroying utopia.[9] The hooded or blindfolded prisoners waited in silence for the next face of pain and were assumed by their torturers as destroyed. However, as the prisoners of the notorious Villa Grimaldi, a prisoner's camp where torture was a daily reality, sat at the only bench that was available, they felt the warmth of others and they could smell the scent of the rosebushes that were located beside the bench.[10] Cold bodies that were underfed dreamt again of a better world and they dreamt to see their families and their loved ones but *only* if, I repeat, *only* if they were able to face their torturers with the dignity of human beings. That dignity remained with the prisoners and the tortured when they kept the power of dreaming, a power that could not be taken away by the fragility of the body and by the ongoing pain of beatings and electricity shocks. However, the prisoners' dreams were communally related to a historical project of changing society and sharing the goods of the earth rather than to personal dreams of possessions or prestige within society.

Within this experience of liberation, utopia is a historical project according to Sheila Cassidy (1992, 300): "The final victory over their terror of pain and physical death is the last of a thousand victories and defeats in the war which is fought daily and hourly in the human mind and soul: the war in the overcoming of self." It is important to realize that the healing of those tortured and those in posttraumatic shock comes not from forgetting the pain and the horror but from the acceptance of it as part of a process of life. In therapies for torture, survivors art and creativity are of the essence to cope with feelings of unworthiness and of loss. In rebuilding the person as a human being loved by God and by others, aesthetic forms realize the possibility of the touch of God in healing the past by revisiting it in different forms. Poetry and writing becomes another form in which the broken person does not forget but assumes the past as unchangeable and the future as full of promise, full of opportunities, and new dreams arise in which the liberating power of the God of Life becomes for those who are members of a faith community the continuity of a human dignity that cannot be taken away, even in death.

Hermeneutical Features

Liberating reflections on unburied bones require the possibility of an action of a God that liberates from suffering and oppression. Thus, I have written somewhere else: "The liberating God of history was in the Villa Grimaldi, not as an all-knowing God who was watching what he already knew... He was there naked on the *parrilla*, on the metallic structure that acted as an electricity conductor, being himself crucified, interrogated and scorned" (Aguilar 2007–2008, vol. II, 111–12).

It is clear that the Christian communities over those years of military regimes supported the relatives of the disappeared in their just cause of knowing what happened to their relatives and who arrested them. The liberating reflections of communities in Latin America and elsewhere exercised love for God and for neighbor in supporting those affected by injustice and what today we call "crimes against humanity." The theological analysis that followed took to heart the findings of many Truth and Reconciliation Commissions that had documented testimonies of the atrocities and that in many cases associated the churches with the defense of the victims.

Theologically, God—the liberating God—has come down from the mountains and the towers of the churches and has become one more victim of arrest, torture, death, and disappearance. Once again the values of the Kingdom of God challenge role models and, within the high theology of the Gospel of John, the crucified draws all things to him (Jn. 12:32, 19:37; Sobrino 2001, 108). In Jon Sobrino's (2001, 109) reflection, the crucified and the victims are the ones who bring salvation, because they are part of a globalized truth of a common humanity drawn by God, rather than part of a humanity that seems to be part of those who have, while "two billion human beings live on less than two dollars a day, half of these on less than one." The excluded of this world are the signs of what Ignacio Ellacuría (1991) calls "the civilization of poverty," a globalized humanity living in common poverty, understood as lacking the basic necessities of life, but living in peace and harmony with each other. Thus, for Sobrino (2001, 109), "placing the suffering of victims at the centre of the 'globe' leads to truth and the universalization of human values. This has nothing to do with 'victim culture' but with the need-invitation to respond to the victims with *mercy and justice.*"

If a renewed liberation theology continues to freshen the liberating presence of God in the Latin American communities, Christians, activists, and liberationists need to resist a break with memory and take the bones and the memories of the disappeared as part of a blueprint of an ongoing liberation theology immersed in the past, present, and future of the victims, thus of the God who liberates. In the words of Jung Mo Sung (2005, 4): "the perspective of the victims must be prominent in such a theological endeavour," and the victims and their families are found in the bones and memories of the victims within the twenty-first century.

Notes

1. See Second General Conference of Latin American Bishops 1968, 1970.
2. For a good historical summary see Klaiber (1998).
3. At the theological level, African and Latin American theologians encountered each other through the Ecumenical Association of Third World Theologians (EATWOT) and the first period of their work was coordinated by Enrique Dussel and François Houtart. See a useful historical overview in Dussel (1984); see also·EATWOT (1976). For a theological overview, see Witvliet (1985). An Asian Christianity as a Christian project was more problematic; numbers of Christians in Asia, with the exception of the Philippines, remain small, and the post-Vatican II discussions on salvation within the world religions created more than an impasse between those who adhered to a Christ centric option (exclusivists) and those who understood the world religions as places where God could save (inclusivists); see Knitter (1985).
4. For a comprehensive history of liberation theology and of some of the most prominent theologians of liberation, see Aguilar (2007–2008).
5. See Aguilar (2009).
6. See Aguilar (2007–2008), vol. II, 97–113.
7. The term "disappeared" became common within the Argentinean dirty war of the 1970s; however, Marguerite Feitlowitz (1998, 51) traces it back to Hitler's orders within the Second World War. Edmundo Murray refers to the founder of *Le Monde*, Hubert Beuve-Méry, who used the terms "dirty war" to refer to the French campaign in Vietnam. Later, "dirty war" and "disappeared" were terms associated with Argentina; however, they were used in connection to the French occupation of Algiers and Vietnam. (Edmundo Murray to H-LATAM email list, August 23, 2006).

8. See the sharp analysis of this historical project within the theology of Gutiérrez in Petrella (2004, 15–16).
9. The role of the churches and of theologians at that time was to reassure Christians of their dignity and of their Christian historical project ignored and despised by the military government; see Aguilar (2004–2009).
10. For the history and practices of torture at the Villa Grimaldi during the years of the military government in Chile, see Aguilar (2000) and Aguilar (2005).

Bibliography

"30 Years on, Mothers Continue to March for Missing Children." *The Times,* December 10, 2005, 54.

Aguilar, M. I. 2000. "El Muro de los Nombres de Villa Grimaldi (Chile): Exploraciones sobre la Memoria, el Silencio y la Voz de la Historia." *European Review of Latin American and Caribbean Studies* 69: 81–88.

———. 2005. "The Ethnography of the Villa Grimaldi in Pinochet's Chile: From Public Landscape to Secret Detention Centre (1973–1980)." *Iberoamericana* 18: 7–23.

———. 2007–2008. *The History and Politics of Latin American Theology*, 3 volumes (vol. II, *Theology and Civil Society*). London: SCM.

———. 2004–2009. *A Social History of the Catholic Church in Chile,* vols. I–V. Lewiston: Edwin Mellen.

———. 2009. *Theology, Liberation and Genocide: A Theology of the Periphery.* London: SCM.

Cassidy, S. 1992. *Audacity to Believe.* London: Darton, Longman and Todd.

Dussel, E. 1984. "Theologies of the 'Periphery' and the 'Centre': Encounter or Confrontation?" In *Different Theologies, Common Responsibility, Babel or Pentecost?* ed. Claude Geffré, Gustavo Gutiérrez, and Virgil Elizondo. *Concilium* 171: 87–97. Edinburgh: T&T Clark.

EATWOT. 1976. *The Emergent Gospel.* Maryknoll: Orbis Books.

Ellacuría SJ, I. 1991. *Veinte años de historia en El Salvador 1969–1989: Escritos políticos*, vol. I. San Salvador: UCA Editores.

Feitlowitz, M. 1998. *A Lexicon of Terror: Argentina and the Legacies of Torture.* New York: Oxford University Press.

Gutiérrez, G. 1985. *A Theology of Liberation: History, Politics and Salvation.* London: SCM.

———. 1993. "Option for the Poor." In *Mysterium Liberationis: Fundamental Concepts of Liberation Theology*, ed. Ignacio Ellacuría, SJ and Jon Sobrino SJ, 235–50. Maryknoll: Orbis Books.

Klaiber, S. J. J. 1998. *The Church, Dictatorships, and Democracy in Latin America.* Maryknoll: Orbis Books.

Knitter, P. F. 1985. *No Other Name? A Critical Survey of Christian Attitudes towards the World Religions.* London: SCM.

Petrella, I. 2004. *The Future of Liberation Theology: An Argument and Manifesto.* Aldershot: Ashgate.

Second General Conference of Latin American Bishops 1968. 1970. *The Church in the Present-Day Transformation of Latin America in the Light of the Council II Conclusions.* Washington, DC: United States Catholic Conference.

Sobrino, J. 2001. "Redeeming Globalization through Its Victims." In *Globalization and Its Victims*, ed. Jon Sobrino and Felix Wilfred. *Concilium* 5: 105–14. London: SCM.

Sung, J. M. 2005. "The Human Being as Subject: Defending the Victims." In *Latin American Liberation Theology: The Next Generation*, ed. Ivan Petrella, 1–19. Maryknoll: Orbis Books.

Wilfred, F. 2007. "Indian Theologies: Retrospect and Prospects, a Sociological Perspective." In *Another Possible World*, ed. Marcella Althaus-Reid, Iván Petrella, and Luiz Carlos Susin, 131–61.

Witvliet, T. 1985. *A Place in the Sun: An Introduction to Liberation Theology in the Third World.* London: SCM.

PART II

United States

CHAPTER 5

A US Theology of Letting Go

Rosemary Radford Ruether

In this essay I want to elucidate some of the basic principles of a US theology of "letting go." I take this term from a small book published in 1977 by sociologist Marie Augusta Neale, titled *A Socio-Theology of Letting Go*. A "theology of letting go" is essentially the complement to theologies of liberation coming from oppressed peoples seeking to throw off oppressive power from hegemonic empires and ruling elites. It is a theology of solidarity between people engaged in particular liberation struggles and their supporters within dominant societies. For those who are oppressed to be liberated, those who hold and exercise oppressive power must "let go" or be made to let go. They must relax their grip on domination so others can go free and build alterative societies. In other words, there must be some repentance on the side of the sinners. Ultimately a transformation of both sides must take place so there is no more poor and rich, oppressed and oppressors, marginalized and privileged but a new society where all members enjoy dignity and access to the basic means of life.

Letting go was at least partially what the South African apartheid regime did or had to do in giving up its dream of two separate societies, white and Black, and allowing equal political citizenship for all in South Africa. Unfortunately this has hardly resulted in a full liberation, but an adjustment of the white ruling class took place, giving up political dominance that was no longer possible, while holding on to economic dominance. Letting go is what the United States has mostly refused to do in relation to the revolutions in the Third World, such as the one in Cuba and in Sandinista Nicaragua, endlessly seeking to undermine and embargo these small nations in order to overthrow their revolutionary regimes.

A theology of letting go addresses the appropriate role of conscientious citizens of imperial nations, specifically in this case the United States, in relation to peoples whom this country is dominating, impoverishing and oppressing, as well as in relation to the more impoverished and oppressed classes and ethnic communities within the United States itself. What is the role of somewhat privileged groups within the United States in responding to theologies of liberation coming from American Blacks, American Indians, from women, especially from poorer groups? What is the role of such privileged groups in relation to theologies of liberation coming from Africa, from Latin America, from Asia, from Palestine? I say somewhat privileged groups, since one hardly expects such a response from the top of the ruling class, which is the font of the problem. One is talking about socially aware and concerned groups in the middle strata of US society who have become aware of the injustices to others and want to find out what it is that they should do about it.

I speak here of a mediating group that struggles against its own government within the imperial nation. There is also a mediating group in more oppressed societies who have come from privileged classes, but who choose to engage in what liberation theology calls the "preferential option for the poor," people like Archbishop Romero in El Salvador, who paid with his life for his option for the poor and his efforts to speak to the wealthy ruling class in his country, as well as to the president of the United States. Liberation theologians have generally come from more educated classes within a society or else from missionaries who dedicated themselves to poor people, such as Jon Sobrino and Ignacio Ellacuria in El Salvador, Jesuit missionaries who came from the Basque region of Spain.

I see those who become advocates of a theology of letting go in a dominant nation as playing a different role from elites in impoverished societies who choose to serve the poor and to develop theologies of liberation. Theologians of letting go are also making a preferential option for the poor, but their role is to become educated in the reality of the oppressed community and also to discover the mechanisms by which oppressive power is exercised in their own society, in order to become critical mediators who press the powerful in their society to let go of supporting particular forms of oppression and to get out of the way of new realities emerging outside their power system. In many cases these mediators within the dominant society also play an important role in helping the liberation spokespersons and movements survive within the oppressed society that is struggling to be free.

These roles of critical mediation within the dominant societies are well known. It is what I and many other colleagues within US critical communities have been doing for more than 40 years. What a theology of letting go does is simply name these roles and seek to articulate its theory and practice in a theological context. This theological context means that it particularly operates out of bases in Christian churches in US society and seeks to speak to members of the churches as a way of educating and seeking to mobilize American society.

I will discuss the role of the Friends of Sabeel in the USA[1] as a way of illustrating the practice and theology of letting go in relation to the oppression of the Palestinian people in the Occupied Territories of the state of Israel, buttressed by the support of the United States. Sabeel is a Palestinian liberation theology movement based in Jerusalem that seeks to change the oppressed status of Palestinians in relation to the state of Israel and create a new just and mutual relation between these two peoples. This struggle for Palestinian liberation, and a new relation of justice and reconciliation between Israelis and Palestinians, entails many elements: (1) overcoming ignorance and falsehood in the dominant media about the situation of Palestinians, (2) criticizing the one sided role of the United States that falsely portrays itself as a "honest broker" between the two communities, (3) knitting together the deeply fragmented Palestinian Christian community, (4) developing working relations of Palestinian Christians and Muslims, as well as (5) between Palestinian Christians and Muslims and Israeli Jews.

Naim Ateek,[2] the founding director and theological spokesman of Sabeel, himself a Palestinian Anglican priest who grew up in Nazareth after his family was expelled from their village in the Jordan Valley by the Israel army in 1948, articulates the main points of the theology of Sabeel. The theology of Sabeel is first, a contextual theology arising from the particular experience of oppression of Palestinians under the state of Israel. Second, it is a liberation theology seeking liberation from this particular situation of injustice. Third, it is an ecumenical and interfaith theology seeking to unite Palestinian Christians and to bring together Christians, Muslims, and Jews to work together for justice and peace in this land. Fourth, it is biblically based, offering a vision of how the Bible points to justice, liberation, and peace in the context of a theology of the land, while also critiquing the fallacious abuse of the Bible by Christian Zionists and Israeli militant settlers. And fifth, it is a theology of nonviolence, rejecting violence as the wrong way to liberation.

The theology of Sabeel developed by Naim Ateek focuses on several key theological issues. Its central question is: What kind of God can we believe in? Is it a racist God who chooses one people against others, or is it a God of justice and love who is the God of all peoples? Sabeel constantly seeks to advocate for an inclusive rather than an exclusive understanding of God. Sabeel sees Jesus Christ as the criterion of interpretation of the Bible for Christians, emphasizing not just his divinity but the fullness of his humanity in his historical context as a Palestinian Jew living under Roman occupation. Sabeel seeks to be followers of Jesus in his way of nonviolent resistance to imperial occupation. Sabeel roots itself in the prophetic theology of the Hebrew Scriptures, standing in the line of the great prophets of ancient Israel in unmasking injustice and calling for a new just society. These prophetic roots also connect them with the other two Abrahamic faiths of Judaism and Islam.

Sabeel develops an anti-imperial theology. It stands in the tradition of the anti-imperial theologies of Hebrew Scripture and the New Testament and applies this critique of ancient empire to modern empires, such as the American empire. It rejects a Son of David imperial Christology, rooting itself instead in a Suffering Servant Christology of the early Church, in its nonviolent way of the cross. It is a theology that aims at reconciliation and peace through a social, economic, and political transformation of relationships between Israel and Palestinians that makes it possible for these people to coexist in genuine justice.

The Friends of Sabeel as an organization of Christians, together with Jews and Muslims, supports the work and vision of Sabeel within European and North American societies. The largest of these is Friends of Sabeel, North America, which includes two groups, one in the United States and one in Canada. There are also groups in the UK, the Republic of Ireland, the Netherlands, and Sweden. I will focus on the work of Friends of Sabeel in the United States, as it is the group to which I belong. Friends of Sabeel in the United States works first of all to make it possible for Sabeel in Palestine to survive. It is a major funding source for Naim Ateek and the Sabeel center in Jerusalem that makes it possible for them to do their work locally, as well as to travel to speak in Europe and North America. Friends of Sabeel seeks to educate US Americans about the Palestinian reality and to counteract the ignorance and distortion that fills the US media about Palestinians, how their oppressed status came about, and how it is being maintained by the state of Israel, particularly through US funding. Friends of Sabeel works through a national coordinating office and a multitude of support groups that develop local conferences and activities. Friends of

Sabeel also lobbies American political leaders, challenging the policy, in its one-sided bias, of the American government toward Israel and the Palestinians.

Theologically Friends of Sabeel endorses Sabeel's theological principles and seeks to communicate this vision to American churches of all denominations. This means developing the critique of Christian Zionism with its false vision of an exclusive God and an election of one people against others and the belief that God gives one people the land of Palestine for all eternity to the exclusion of other people historically part of this land. It repudiates the apocalypticism that calls Christians to look forward to a coming Armageddon that will destroy all other peoples other than God's elect Christians with select Jewish converts. It also seeks to counteract the apathy of mainstream Christian churches that keep silent in the face of Palestinian oppression and endorse in more subtle way a theology that justifies exclusive Jewish domination of the land from the perspective of the ideas of election, chosenness, the promised land, and recompense for the Christian guilt for the Holocaust. This does not mean that Western Christians should not repent of Christian anti-Semitism; they should. But they should not use such repentance to ignore new crimes, such as the ethnocide of the Palestinian people.

Although Friends of Sabeel is an ecumenical Christian movement, it is also interfaith, with representatives of the Muslim and Jewish communities regularly speaking at their conferences. In recent years more and more critical Jewish spokespersons, both Israeli and American, have emerged, such as Jeff Halper, head of the committee against housing demolition in Israel, and Anna Baltzer, a leading spokesperson for justice for the Palestinians based on her own experience. Many other American Jews and Jewish movements critical of Israeli policy have found a home in Sabeel that supports them and welcomes their collaboration.

The theology of Friends of Sabeel, while rooting itself in Sabeel's Palestinian liberation theology, also applies it as a theology of solidarity with the Palestinians in the North American context. Thus it challenges the way many American Christians adhere to Christian Zionist types of theology and tacitly accept ideas of an exclusivist God and promised land, often in a way that privilege a unique alliance of Israel and America as divinely elect peoples. It directs its critique and call for a new vision and practice to their own US government, which is the major power that makes it possible for this unjust situation in Israel to continue. It calls on the United States to let go of its imperial policies in the Middle East, and its use of Israel as a tool of that imperial policy,

and to allow Israelis and Palestinians, as well as the other peoples of
the Middle East, to forge more just, peaceful, and ecologically sustainable relations with each other, seeking a more just sharing of the vital
resources of land, water, and oil in Israel-Palestine.

Notes

1. See the North American website http://www.fosna.org for further details.
2. A list of his books is included in the bibliography.

Bibliography

Ateek, N. 1989. *Justice and Only Justice: A Palestinian Theology of Liberation.*
Maryknoll: Orbis Books.
———. 2008. *A Palestinian Christian Cry for Reconciliation.* Maryknoll: Orbis
Books.
Friends of Sabeel North America Homepage: http://www.fosna.org, accessed 17
January 2012.
Neale, M. A. 1977. *A Socio-Theology of Letting Go: The Role of a First World Church
Facing Third World Peoples.* New York: Paulist.
Raheb, M. 1995. *I am a Palestinian Christian.* Minneapolis: Fortress.
———. 2004. *Bethlehem Besieged: Stories of Hope in Times of Trouble* Minneapolis:
Fortress.
Ruether, R., and H. Ruether. 2002. *The Wrath of Jonah: The Crisis of Religious
Nationalism in the Israeli-Palestinian Conflict,* 2nd edition. Minneapolis:
Fortress.
Zaru, J. 2008. *Occupied with Non-Violence: A Palestinian Woman Speaks.*
Minneapolis: Fortress.

CHAPTER 6

Dialogic Mediations: Reflections on the Hopeful Future of US Liberation Theology

Benjamín Valentín
bvalentin@ants.edu

A t present, and for some time now, many have been asking questions about the prospects and future of liberation theology, and for good reasons too. After all, liberation theology has been around for about 40 years now. In terms of the academy, that could just as well be counted in "dog years" due to the academy's penchant for the latest thing: yesterday liberation theology; today postcolonial theology; tomorrow who knows? But, besides this matter of age or "long-history," if it can be called that, there is also the fact that the historical context of liberation theology has changed much in the course of those 40 plus years. We are probably all informed of the pertinent changes by now, but it might still be worth mentioning the resistance that liberation theology has met with in certain sectors of the church: the decline of mainline liberal churches and the expansion of conservative mega-churches and of charismatic and holiness movements that are not always receptive to liberation theology; the entrenchment of capitalism as both an economic and cultural system; the internationalization of corporations; the fragmentation of the political and religious Left; the silent deepening of a racial, ethnic, and class divide; the loss of a sense of the thoroughly relational character of the web of life; and the narrowed sense of public purpose and political possibility that marks contemporary public life and thought, among other things.

These circumstances and developments have either emerged or intensified more recently, combining to make the task, mission, and vision of liberation theology that much harder to achieve and fathom. And the truth is that liberation theologians have been slow in responding to these newer or resurgent circumstances and challenges. On account of this, and on account of the circumstances I have just mentioned, some have taken to the writing off of liberation theology or to the announcement of its demise, decline, or obsolescence. This is understandable: the contextual conditions are dreary and vexing; the social, political, economic, cultural, and ecclesiastical forecast disheartening; and the challenge for present-day theorists and advocates of change and social justice is palpably arduous. And yet, some of us continue to believe that liberation theology or at least "something like" liberation theology is needed for the twenty-first century and beyond—and by this I mean a theological program that roots out and contends with patterns of injustice; empowers ordinary people; and promotes progressive social movements for change, all while putting forward religious theories or theologies that can orient human activity toward personal fulfillment and greater social justice. But what initiatives, what directions, and what correctives should liberation theology engage and bring into play if it is to be meaningful and effectual in the new landscape of the twenty-first century? These are fair questions. And so, in the following pages, I want to enumerate and shed light upon three paths or goals that I would like to see us US liberationists pursue.

Consolidating Recognition and Redistribution: Toward a Broader Emancipatory Political Vision and Project

The first of my aspirations involves the merging of two analytically distinct conceptions of injustice: the first being socioeconomic injustice, which has to do with inequity that is rooted in and results from the political and economic structuring of society, and the second being cultural injustice, which has to do with inequity that is rooted in and results from social patterns of valuation and representation.[1] For a while now I have been noting and saying that we US liberation theologians have mostly tended to focus our attention on cultural or symbolic injustice and nothing has happened in more recent years to make me change my mind about this reading of US liberation theology. In other words, my sense is that, whether by design or not, we have devoted most of our energies on the task of addressing and contesting oppressions that have to do with cultural domination, nonrecognition, and disrespect. For that reason one will notice that we have made the discovery, defense, celebration, and reconstruction of cultures and identities; the recognition of difference, whether of nationality, ethnicity, race, gender, or sexuality; and the fight against assimilationist tendencies and/or hurtful stereotypic public representations a central aim in our theologies. And this I say is a good thing and a necessary thing. These concerns and struggles are valid and have everything to do with justice, and they must continue to be part of any emancipatory project and, therefore, of US liberation theology.

What is unfortunate, however, is that the focus on matters of cultural or symbolic injustice has apparently served to divert our attention away from issues that are related to socioeconomic injustice. Whether for this reason or others, we can note that injustices corresponding to exploitation, economic marginalization, and deprivation have received less attention in our theologies. For sure, we encounter some works and plenty of brief statements here and there that mention and denounce the mal-distributive effects of capitalism, poverty, and other such socioeconomic problems. But, in all honesty, we must admit that solid socioeconomic analysis has not been a strong point in US liberation theology. It is one thing to mention and denounce these social and economic conditions in passing or in vague form. It is quite another to devote a good deal of attention to them by way of careful and sustained analysis of their causes, conditions, and prospects for remediation. I suggest that we should look to connect our concerns and demands for cultural change to an equally resolute, principled, and well-reasoned concern and demand for socioeconomic change. And we must do so in good part because the reality is that many people in our social groups, communities, and society continue to suffer injustices that are traceable to both political economy and to culture simultaneously. So, as I look forward to the import of US liberation theology in the twenty-first century, I envision the construction of theological colloquies that can tie together the problematics of recognition and redistribution and can, in this way, adopt the cause of a more comprehensive emancipatory project for justice.

Caring about the Quality of Our Lives Together: Toward a Coalitional Spirit

My second point and longing calls for the building and nourishment of wider communal bonds among different communities of struggle. A point at issue that we liberationists must recognize, deal with, and speak to is the fracturing of the political Left, or what I like to refer to as "the fracturing of utopian energies along group lines of difference."

In the post-Civil Rights era we have seen not a vacuum of movements for change but actually the emergence of various movements for change, each politicizing a specific difference in order to contest one or another form of subordination. Whether they be feminist, African-American, Native American, Chicano/Chicana, Hispanic/Latino(a), Asian American, GLBTQ, or ecological, these different movements have generally found themselves sharing political space with each other in the general society and in the academy but not sharing parallel or coalesced existence. No doubt that all of these movements have been needed in society and in the academy. And there is no doubt that each of these social groups and movements has helped to procure some level of justice, at times gaining their advocates localized victories. Still, if we are honest, we will admit that these various movements for change have often cut across one another. They have also tended to turn inward toward their own concerns and causes, often ignoring the possibility and desirability of coalition—of action on many fronts for social change. To be sure, we must grant that this inward turn is not only understandable but also required, inasmuch as each social group and movement must go through a process of discovering experiences, differences, and needs within itself.

Be that as it may, one can recognize that the kind of substantive change that these groups and movements desire in the cultural and social realms requires, at least every now and again, the achievement of coalitions of struggle across racial, ethnic, gender, class, and other lines of difference. For that reason we should yearn for collaborative political activity from time to time. But collaborative political activity, solidarities of difference, and strategic alliances and coalitions do not just happen; rather, they require a certain kind of awareness, mindfulness, willingness, effort, and promotion. That is, they require recognition of the common good that undergirds our communal, national, and global destinies; they require that we care about the quality of our lives together; they require a willingness to engage each other in conversation; they require a concerted effort to search for and pursue shared interests and ends; and they require a willingness to throw light upon the interstitial sites of interaction, interconnection, and exchange that may exist between our different spaces of identity and struggle. In these days of increasing inequality, continuing discrimination, sociopolitical fragmentation, and fashionable localism, there is a definite need for discourse that can articulate a broad enough emancipatory vision and can pull people beyond boundaries of difference to work toward collective goals. This exigency presents liberation theology with a challenge and an opportunity.[2]

Getting Back to Theology and Religious Theory: Toward a Theological Imagination

My third and final point and longing calls for a return to the generation of constructive theologies and religious theories. I have noticed that in the last two decades or so much discussion within liberation theology has remained bogged down in the question of theological method or the question of appropriate models for the study of practiced religion. It also appears that the theological concerns of more recent liberationist theologians have veered heavily toward sociocultural and political analysis and cultural critique. One could say that recent writings in US liberation theology evince a kind of theological evasion—that is, a refusal or at least hesitancy to engage in serious theological reflection and construction. As a result, our writings end up reading more like prolegomena to theology or like hurried social and political commentaries than like writings in theology that serve to open new discursive space in our theological work. I applaud, and I personally have contributed to, this turn toward methodological inquiry, sociocultural analysis, and historical and political commentary in theology. And I do think that we must continue this sort of work. In fact, I think we liberation theologians need to immerse ourselves even deeper into the waters of social, political, cultural, and economic theory to make sure we are well equipped to respond to the complex challenges of our time in an informed and intelligent manner. However, I lament the kind of theological evasion that has surfaced among us. And I think we need to remind ourselves that we are in fact theologians and religious scholars. That being so, our task is not only that of commenting on past and current affairs and that of commenting on issues of social justice or injustice but also that of producing constructive theologies and religious theories. We must, therefore, continue to interpret, reexamine, and reshape theological symbols and doctrines in the light of our justice concerns and in the light of our historical, cultural, social, political, and economic analysis. Theology is certainly made up of many subdisciplines and can incorporate many reflective quests. Never to be forgotten among these tasks, however, is the task of interpreting, evaluating, and expounding upon the religious symbols or doctrinal concepts that make up the Christian tradition. This includes the effort to interpret, to evaluate, and to reformulate the meanings of themes, symbols, or doctrines such as God, Creation, human nature, human sin, Christ, the church, and eschatology, for instance. As theologians we cannot evade the onus of a more systematic and reconstructive treatment of these basic symbols, themes, and doctrines. Just the same, we must continue to bring forward religious theories and to highlight the religious dimensions of culture and life in a creative and constructive manner. And we must continue to aim for the provision of timely strategies for personal meaning, the sustenance of people through the traumas of life, the emboldening of a moral sensibility, and the fostering of hope for a tomorrow that transcends the present. These aspirations come with the vocation of the theologian, and perhaps especially the vocation of the liberation theologian in these challenging and demoralizing times. And it should be clear that these aspirations call for constructive and visionary theological work.

To be sure, I am not suggesting that we liberation theologians need to choose between the pursuit of constructive theological work and the calling of social theory, cultural criticism, and historical analysis. My suggestion is that we fasten these pursuits together, not allowing the demands of one (that is, the exigency of rigorous social, cultural, political, economic, and historical analysis) to undermine the mandates of the other (that is, the requirement of systematic or constructive theological work, which implies the need to continue to reexamine and reshape the symbols and doctrines of Christian theology).

This was one of the achievements of early liberation theologians, and I believe it is one reason why we continue to read, study, and speak about them today. I think, for example, of Gustavo Gutiérrez's stimulating reinterpretation of the notion of salvation, Jon Sobrino's rethinking of the nature and tasks of Christology, James Cone's theological interpretation of the spirituals and blues, Mary Daly's philosophical reflections on the nature and power of theological language, Rosemary Radford Ruether's feminist systematic theology, Leonardo Boff's novel rendering of the social implications of the Trinity, Delores Williams' reformulation of atonement, and Ivone Gebara's refreshing mysticism and presentation of a relational transcendence.[3] These all provide examples of constructive theological efforts and works originating in the 1970s, 1980s, and 1990s. These also provide examples of constructive theological efforts that combined critical theory and theological study. Constructive or reconstructive work like this is still created by us liberationists today, at least from time to time.[4] But my sense is that it is in much shorter supply. And I am simply suggesting that we can add to our theological ingenuity by exploring the possible meanings and applicability of the different symbols, concepts, and doctrines of our religious traditions more often and in a more methodical and intentional manner. And this we must try to do while not dispensing with the social and cultural theory and the political, economic, and historical analysis that is necessary in and unique to our "liberationist" intellectual offerings.

Concluding Remarks

So, in closing, in answer to the question of what liberation theologies should represent in the twenty-first century, I respond that it is my hope that they will be discourses that speak equally to issues of recognition and redistribution, promote and provide the basis for collaborative enterprises, and put forth fresh interpretations and reformulations of theological themes in the light of the conditions of life in our postmodern and postsocialist era.

Notes

1. My conceptual and discursive framework here draws upon Nancy Fraser's critical social theory. See Fraser (1997), Fraser (2003), and Fraser (2009).
2. For more on the importance, exigencies, and prospects of coalitional activism, see Valentín (2002), esp. 74–80 and 107–16.
3. See Gutiérrez (1973), Sobrino (1993), Cone (1972), Daly (1973), Ruether (1983), Boff (1988), Williams (1993), and Gebara (1999).
4. Two recent authors who appear, in my view, to have bucked this trend of theological evasion and have put forth refreshing and intellectually or theoretically rich constructive theological works that are still firmly grounded in liberation theology are Marcella Althaus-Reid and Mayra Rivera. See, for example, Althaus-Reid (2000, 2003, 2011) and Rivera (2007).

Bibliography

Althaus-Reid, M. 2000. *Indecent Theology: Theological Perversions in Sex, Gender, and Politics.* New York: Routledge.
———. 2003. *The Queer God.* New York: Routledge.
———. 2011. *From Feminist Theology to Indecent Theology.* London: SCM.
Boff, L. 1988. *Trinity and Society.* Maryknoll: Orbis Books.
Cone, J. 1972. *The Spirituals and Blues: An Interpretation.* New York: Seabury.
Daly, M. 1973. *Beyond God the Father: Toward a Philosophy of Women's Liberation.* Boston: Beacon.
Fraser, N. 1997. *Justice Interruptus: Critical Reflections on the "Postsocialist" Condition.* New York: Routledge.
———. 2003. *Redistribution or Recognition? A Political-Philosophical Exchange.* New York: Verso.
———. 2009. *Scales of Justice: Reimagining Political Space in a Globalizing World.* New York: Columbia University Press.

Gebara, I. 1999. *Longing for Running Water: Ecofeminism and Liberation.* Minneapolis: Fortress.

Gutiérrez, G. 1973. *A Theology of Liberation: History, Politics, and Salvation.* Maryknoll: Orbis Books.

Rivera, M. 2007. *The Touch of Transcendence: A Postcolonial Theology of God.* Louisville: Westminster John Knox.

Ruether, R. R. 1983. *Sexism and God-Talk: Toward a Feminist Theology.* Boston: Beacon.

Sobrino, J. 1993. *Jesus the Liberator: A Historical Theological Reading of Jesus of Nazareth.* Maryknoll: Orbis Books.

Valentín, B. 2002. *Mapping Public Theology: Beyond Culture, Identity, and Difference.* Harrisburg: Trinity Press International.

Williams, D. 1993. *Sisters in the Wilderness: The Challenge of Womanist God-Talk.* Maryknoll: Orbis Books.

CHAPTER 7

American Indian Liberation: Paddling a Canoe Upstream

Tink Tinker

I recall my second visit to the site of the 1864 Sand Creek Massacre to honor Cheyenne and Arapaho people, and especially the peace chiefs, who had died in that unprovoked and murderous surprise attack on their peaceful village. Just after midnight, several hours before a dawn ceremony, two of us walked out from the cottonwoods at the old village site in the hollow at the bend of the creek bed and ventured into the prairie a couple of hundred yards. As we stood under the light of the moon, we were quietly stunned by the sounds of a large and busy village coming from the cottonwoods. In the middle of this semi-arid Colorado ranchland, miles from the nearest town and more than a mile from the nearest house, we distinctly heard children playing, dogs barking, neighing horses, men singing around a drum, people calling to each other. It reminded me of my first visit two years earlier, on the anniversary of the Massacre.

On that earlier visit four of us had trekked to the site for a sunrise prayer ceremony to remember the hundreds who had been murdered. The temperature was 30 degrees below freezing and there was a fresh four-inch coat of snow on the ground, similar to conditions reported for the day that the Reverend (Col.) Chivington initiated his ill-trained U.S. Army unit's vicious preemptive attack on the unsuspecting Cheyenne and Arapaho families that were just beginning to stir.[1] Ours was the only car in the parking area and the only tracks in the new snow as we began to walk through the icy cold. By the time the sun had begun to rise above the horizon, we had walked beyond the cottonwoods out into the expanse of the prairie and had filled a no^nnio^nba (a prayer pipe) and sung a ceremonial song to the pipe and to the ancestors there to ask for their help. Then as we each in turn took the pipe to speak our prayers, I noticed an Indian woman about 60 yards to the south, praying with her face to the sunrise. She was dressed in a black skirt or dress, wrapped in a red shawl, and had long black hair braided down her back. I watched her while we prayed until finally, as we smoked the pipe to finish our prayers, I looked up again and noticed that she was gone just as suddenly as she had appeared—leaving no tracks in the snow.

These two stories recall experiences, personal and communal, that have helped to shape my own understanding of the world. Any American Indian articulation of a theology will necessarily be constructed on the foundation of experience. I want to use these two narratives as the starting point for my own expression of an American Indian liberation theology—because they capture something that runs deep in the experience of Indian communities—both in terms of our awareness of our own history as recipients of injustice and violence and the experience of the sacred.

The classic liberation theologies have always been explicitly political. The liberation of oppressed and poor people must struggle with the role that political systems play in maintaining oppression. So too, American Indian perspectives on liberation must be nothing short of explicitly political. American Indians are far and away, the poorest of the poor in north America, consistently oppressed and suppressed politically, socially, psychologically, economically—with ramifications that manifest themselves in our physical and mental health and in our spiritual well-being as well.

Yet, both the cultural particularities of American Indian communities and the particularities of Indian experiences of colonization and conquest mandate a different approach to American Indian liberation theology. American Indians represent cultures and communities that predate the euro-western invasion of the Americas by thousands of generations. We were people who knew the spiritual side of all life, who had firm experiential connections with the spirit world and the fundamental power of all life, who had well-developed ceremonies to help us maintain harmony and balance in the life of our communities and the world around us. We were communities of peace, most of whom did not even have words for war.[2] Indeed, the language of war became the jargon of states and their technologies of control, something inimical to Indian nations in north America. Thus any Indian liberation theology must begin with the specifics of Indian cultures and cultural values.

The "classic" liberation theologies read in north America begin with the people—that is, with the "experience" of the poor and oppressed—and then move decidedly toward a people's liberating interpretation of Jesus and the gospel. For American Indians, to the contrary, the radical interpretation of Jesus would be an unproductive starting point for a liberation theology since the first proclamation of Jesus among any Indian community came as the beginning of a colonial conquest that included the total displacing of centuries-old religious traditions and the replacing of those traditions with the imposition of a one-size-fits-all euro-western Jesus.[3] Embracing a radical Jesus means nevertheless embracing to some degree the evil perpetrated against our ancestors by those who first brought Jesus to us and engaged in the colonization and conquest of our peoples and our lands. We recall that Junípero Serra had canons fired to demonstrate spanish military power as he "celebrated" his first mass among Native People in California.

We must look for another—a more unconventional and much more complex starting point for a Native liberation theology. Let me describe four aspects of the beginnings of an American Indian liberation theology, which must build upon the tensions between Indian peoples and missionary Christianity, on the peculiarities of israelite history with regard to those tensions, on the cultural abrasiveness of colonially imposed categories of cognition that derive from missionizing evangelism (past and present), and on the renaissance of Indian traditional culture and ceremonial life as a source of revivification and uniquely Indian source of liberation.

Tensions with Christianity

The tensions between Christianity and Indian peoples derives first of all from those notions of amer-european christian triumphalism, christian uniqueness, the proclaimed necessity of salvation according to the european missionary message, and the concomitant sense of euro-western and amer-european superiority.

From a liberated/decolonized Indian perspective, an Indian liberation theology must recognize the source of our bondage and thereby acknowledge a long and tension filled relationship with Christianity as the religion of our colonizer, remembering its missionaries imposing themselves on our peoples. Today, all Indian people have been touched in some way by these missionary processes. Many have converted, some out of genuine desire to be like our White relatives, others out of some perceived necessity to placate the colonizer.[4]

While many traditional spiritual leaders on our reservations today are quick to affirm Jesus as a deeply spiritual person historically, they are also apt to denounce the historical and contemporary function of the church as one of the key factors in the devastation of their own communities. The problem is not Jesus but, rather, the particularity of the missionary preaching of Jesus. To this extent, missionaries worked through the institutional structures, and always imposed particular sorts of institutionalized and nationalist types of Christianity, and were thus always participating in the genocide of Indian peoples in one way or another. Whether Indian persons find liberation through accepting and adapting some version of Christianity or rejecting it outright, these issues of religious conquest and religious colonialism must be acknowledged.

Exchanging Histories: Canaanites, Cowboys, and Indians[5]

In terms of constructing any "christian" liberation theology for American Indians, one must reconcile the claims that two conflicting histories make on Indian peoples' lives. One of the curious oddities of euro-christianity relates to its canonical inclusion of the hebrew bible, which results in necessarily forcing all adherents to embrace a history that is not the natural or actual history of the persons or peoples who become adherents—unless they are "Jews for Jesus." Appropriating a foreign history as one's own means the denial of one's own proper history. For American Indians it means, for instance, the denial of important aspects of our own history in order to affirm not only israelite history but ultimately also amer-euro-christian history.

More significantly, for American Indians, affirming israelite history means ultimately affirming precisely that historical narrative that has been used consistently by our euro-western colonizer to validate their own theft of our property and murder of our ancestors. As Robert Warrior has demonstrated, the puritan invaders' use of the Exodus narrative of ancient Israel's escape from slavery and their divinely mandated conquest of someone else's land, namely, the land of Canaan, empowered the puritan colonial invasion of Indian lands and justified in their minds the murder of Indian people. The same narrative gives birth to the religio-political doctrine of "manifest destiny" and all contemporary religious and political forms of american exceptionalism. For American Indians, Warrior (1989) reminds us forcefully, the conquest narrative is one in which we always discover ourselves to be the Canaanites, the conquered, and never the israelites. Moreover, for Indian Peoples our history is intimately linked to our land, land that has been alienated from us by the christian invasion of the New Israel.

Imposition of the Colonizer's Categories of Cognition

Any Indian notion of liberation must attempt to break away from the conventions of language used so easily and comfortably by our colonizer. The christian invaders' imaginary, established by invasion and conquest, have become the "first principles" and are infused throughout the colonizer's language about religion, theology, politics, and even the simplest realities of everyday life—from euro-christian individualism to images of the sacred Other that the colonizer calls "god" with a capital G and then invests with particular anthropomorphic characteristics. These aspects of christian colonialist languaging imposed on the conquered include the following partial list:

1. Teaching American Indians to value the *private ownership of property* as a means of inculcating individualism became a battle cry for those american religious and political leaders who would "civilize" Indians in the late nineteenth century.[6] We, whose cultural values are based on community, were explicitly and forcibly taught to say "mine" instead of "ours" and "me" instead of "us."
2. The traditional *ecumenical creeds* of euro-western Christianity are deeply rooted in the categories of late classical (hellenistic) greek philosophy, of stoicism and middle platonism, and all euro-christian theology since has built implicitly or explicitly on these categorical distinctions. To an American Indian the words can have little meaning at all within our cultural frames of reference. Spirit and substance are antithetical notions for Indian peoples—at least they are antithetical in our sense of the reciprocal dualism of spirit and matter. *wako^{n}da*, the sacred other, the primordial creative force—but certainly not god, whatever this thing is— that Indians conceive of as spirit or energy. This means, to talk about god as having "substance" is, for us, bizarre at best.
3. Another aspect of missionary Christianity that is destined to be forever difficult for Indian people is the euro-western religious language of *fall and redemption*. Sin is the universal starting point in the euro-christian religious proclamation, with salvation in Jesus posited in some form as the answer to the problem of sin and fall.[7] Its pervasive result is a depreciated level of self-esteem that all too readily internalizes any missionary preaching that intends

first to convict people of their sin. The end result is that for both groups, Indian "sinfulness" is seen as somehow connected to their racial/ethnic identity.

Unfortunately by the time the preacher gets to the "good news" of the gospel, people are so bogged down in their experience and internalization of brokenness and lack of self-worth that too often they never quite hear any proclamation of "good news" in any actualized, existential sense. Any Indian theoretical notion of the world and the role of human beings in it would begin with the world as a complex interrelationship of life. This means that a First Article/Creation starting point might form a more natural bond with indigenous cultural roots.

4. If the convert is required to adopt israelite history, on the one hand, it becomes an important part of the conversion experience for Indian people to *adopt european history* as well. If one is to become a "theologian" in my institution, it is not enough to know indigenous theology, but one must be at least well-enough versed to put it into the framework of nineteenth- and twentieth-century european thinkers, from Schleiermacher to Barth.

In this regard, Indian Christians, and other indigenous Christians, are destined to be forever "one down" because they are not native speakers of or educated in the technical languages of Christianity—greek, hebrew, latin, german, and so on—and neither are they as comfortably conversant in the cultural-linguistic concepts almost automatically presumed by euro-western Christians. And if an Indian becomes a scholar with intense language skills and resources, it always seems as if we lose that person to a deeply acculturated and possibly assimilated status within White church or White society.

5. Even traditional liberation theologies' radical resistance language—like the *"preferential option for the poor"*—can become just another example of imposed language. While the concept is attractive in one sense, it sets priorities that are not ours but imposed by others.

Indian people are the poorest ethnic community in north America. Yet the language of "option for the poor" is nearly meaningless language for Indians. "The poor" as a category presumes a radically non-Indian world of social hierarchy, socioeconomic organization, and a social class structure that are all foreign to traditional Indian communities. Furthermore, it implies a socialist analysis and proposed solution that is completely at odds with American Indian aspirations. As I have argued in an earlier essay (1994), Indian people want affirmation not as "persons" (Gutiérrez' language) or as individuals, but rather as national communities with discrete cultures, discrete languages, discrete value systems, and our own governments and territories.

Cultural alterity becomes primary for any indigenous community. While indigenous peoples would form a more-or-less united front of resistance against capitalism, euro-western notions of representative democracy, the forces of globalization, and amer-european hegemony in general, there has never been an indigenous rush to marxist-style class analysis or political notions of socialism. The goal of every indigenous community is to be recognized as a community, as a cultural whole distinct from the colonial settler hordes who have surrounded us, murdered our ancestors, stolen our property, forced their education on our peoples, and made every attempt to deny us the cultural continuity of language and community solidarity.

In sum, while the claim for liberation can play on christian and biblical themes, these are not *our* themes or *our* language. We will have to look elsewhere for freedom.

Liberating Renaissance of Indian Traditional Religious Structures

The liberation track that I will argue here is one that affirms the "old covenant" promises that were given to Indian peoples when the people were taught (and are being taught) traditional ceremonial ways. This presumes that those ways and ceremonial traditions are still good and appropriate for Indian peoples. When my brother decided some years ago to bring the sun dance back to the Osage people, it was a clear liberative act with deep theological implications for the Osage Nation. The revival of the sun dance is indicative of a larger movement among Indian peoples to reclaim the religious traditions and ceremonies that were denied to us by the missionaries and even by federal policy and actual legal interdiction.

Nearly two decades ago, I suggested that christian Indians need to think of our traditional Indian cultures—with their rich stories and powerful ceremonies—as part of an "old testament" tradition that might become for Indian Christians the only appropriate foundation for affirming Jesus and expressing a christian commitment.[8] These traditions need to be respected as gifts from the spirit world to help people achieve balance and harmony in the world. We think it is time to recognize that this thing that our christian relatives call god has, and has had historically, multiple relationships in the world with huge varieties of peoples and cultures all over the world, even at that moment when the Jesus event was emerging in Palestine two millennia ago.

One possible Indian response, then, that would take their christian conversion and commitments seriously, would be to insist that we Indian people must be free to interpret the gospel for ourselves, even constructing an interpretation of Jesus on the "old" testament foundation of ancient tribal traditions. We could argue that an interpretation of Galatians 5:1 gives Indian peoples the freedom "in Christ" to continue to practice their ancient and traditional ceremonies and rites. "For Christ has made you free" ought to allow for a great variety of religious experience. Some of us have asked missionaries and bishops alike, exactly how free are Indian people to pray the way they want or have for generations?

Indian people who are serious about liberation—about freedom and independence—must commit themselves to the renewal and revival of their tribal ceremonial life, bringing their ancient ceremonies back into the center of their community's political existence. It may be important to live these traditions quite apart from any attempt to force them into some indigenous pattern of Christianity. While there are numerous examples of small groups within nearly every reservation community who have made the move back to their ancient traditions, seldom has this movement embraced the whole of a national community in such a way that the ceremonies have become once again the spiritual base for the political cohesiveness of an independent nation.

To say "Jesus is the answer" is to assume a euro-western question to begin with—to say nothing of the hegemony of the amer-european denominational structures that direct mission activities on reservations. How is Jesus the answer to the intentional destruction of our Indian cultures and languages—perpetrated by missionaries first of all? More to the point, what is it that Jesus might offer our peoples in addition to the life promised in the regular completion of certain ceremonies? And what compromises must we Indians make in order to affirm Jesus as our own? Will we have to concede the intrinsic goodness of our colonial invaders, and finally concede the historical thefts of our property?

After five hundred years of conquest and missionary imposition, it seems time for Indian communities to resuscitate their old, communal ways of relating to the world around them and particularly to relate to the world of the spirits to find life for the peoples in those ceremonial ways and cultural values.

Ceremonial Revivification and New Age Colonialists

While the revivification of Indian tribal ceremonies must be seen as a source of healing and liberation for Indian peoples, these traditions must be understood within the parameters of Indian national cultures and dare not be suddenly interpreted/misinterpreted within the context of the colonizers cultural traditions and values. In the aftermath of christian conquest and colonialism, the cultural values inherent in ceremonial traditions such as the sun dance are shifting noticeably away from the communitarian values of "dancing for the people," "that the people might live." As more and more non-Indian relatives invade our ceremonies, the values have shifted to address the needs and cultural values of these tourists. The sun dance is increasingly danced for the purpose of personal (individual) achievement, a new and exotic source of individual salvation and personal empowerment. I would encourage our amer-european relatives to find another way to find their own center of balance.

An Indian Challenge to Our amer-european Colonizer Relatives

We understand that our liberation is not possible without the liberation of our White relatives who share this continent with us. Indian Peoples stand as a source of judgment over against the continued amer-european occupancy of north America and will always present Americans with a choice: either confess and acknowledge that history and move beyond it in a constructive healing way, or engage the addict's device of denial (i.e., dry-drunk behavior) and keep those memories deeply suppressed and repressed where they will continue to fester and disrupt all of american life and well-being.

An American Indian theology of liberation, then, will hold the colonizer to his and her own best spiritual and moral imperatives:

- Thus, in the name of Jesus we call on all White Christians to *confess*—to acknowledge the american history of violence: violence as military genocide, as political genocide, as cultural genocide, and particularly as the spiritual genocide of missionary conquest.
- And in the name of Jesus we call on all White Christians to *cease and desist* from any attempts to impose their beliefs on others.
- In the name of Jesus, we call on our White relatives to *resist judgment* of our religious and ceremonial traditions.
- Instead, we call on our White relatives to *reflect deeply and honestly* on their own history and its contemporary manifestations in the

form of mass consumption, commodification, the globalization of capital, and the establishment of a new world empire predicated on White american hegemony.

Challenges for Indian People

I also want to end this essay by calling on Indian people to take their cultures and traditions seriously. If we want to be free and want our grandchildren to be free, then there are things we need to do in order to secure a liberated future and to break away from the bondage we have experienced under the tutelage of amer-european values, education, economics, and politics.

- *Culture is lived* by people and not something preserved in museums.
- Our movement for liberation must be a *spiritual movement* as much as it is political.
- Our traditional spirituality and cultural values must *become a real part of everything* we do as Indian persons, political action groups, in our ceremonies, and especially as Indian communities.
- Liberation is *freedom to practice, recover, restore, reinvent* whatever tribal/indigenous practices and lifeways are enriching, healing, and life-sustaining.
- Each one of us should strive to be *personally in balance* but always focused on the balance of our whole community.
- Affirmation of our own cultural values must accompany a *commitment to live those values* in the face of forces that insist on an increasingly globalized culture of commodification and consumption.

These are the commitments to liberation we owe to the memory of those Indian ancestors who gave so much in the colonial contest that resulted in the loss of our lands and the loss of so many lives during the last 520 years.

Notes

1. The best books on the Sand Creek Massacre (1864) are Hoig (1961) and Kelman (2013). For a fuller picture of the persistence of colonial violence in the Americas, see Churchill (1997).
2. See Jaimes and Halsey (1992). On the use of lies and illegalities to secure the amer-european theft of lands, see Churchill (1993).
3. See Tinker (1993).

4. See chapter five in Tinker (1993).
5. This sub-title is borrowed from Warrior (1989).
6. See Prucha (1973).
7. See Tinker (1989).
8. My notion here was picked up by Steve Charleston (Choctaw), then on the faculty at Luther Theological Seminary in St. Paul, MN. See Charleston (1990).

Bibliography

Charleston, S. 1990. "The Old Testament of Native America." In *Lift Every Voice: Constructing Christian Theologies from the Underside*, ed. Susan Brooks Thistlethwaite and Mary Potter Engle, 49–61. New York: Harper and Row.

Churchill, W. 1993. *Struggle for the Land*. Monroe: Common Courage.

———. 1997 *A Little Matter of Genocide: Holocaust and Denial in the Americas, 1492 to the Present*. San Francisco: City Lights Books.

Hoig, S. 1961. *The Sand Creek Massacre*. Oklahoma City: University of Oklahoma Press.

Jaimes, M. A., and T. Halsey. 1992. "American Indian Women: At the Center of Indigenous Resistance in North America." In *The State of Native America: Genocide, Colonization and Resistance*, ed. M Annette Jaimes, 311–44. Boston: South End.

Kelman, A. 2013. *A Misplaced Massacre: Struggling over the Memory of Sand Creek*. Cambridge: Harvard University Press.

Prucha, F. P. 1973. *Americanizing the American Indian: Writings of the Friends of the Indian, 1880–1900*. Cambridge: Harvard University Press.

Tinker, T. 1989. "The Integrity of Creation: Restoring Trinitarian Balance." *Ecumenical Review*, 41: 527–36.

———. 1993. *Missionary Conquest: The Gospel and Native American Genocide*. Minneapolis: Fortress.

———. 1994. "Spirituality, Native American Personhood, Sovereignty and Solidarity." In *Spirituality of the Third World. A Cry for Life*, Papers and Reflections from the Third General Assembly of the Ecumenical Association of Third World Theologians, January 1992, Nairobi, Kenya, ed. K. C. Abraham and B. Mbuy-Beya, 119–32. Maryknoll: Orbis Books.

Warrior, R. 1989. "Canaanites, Cowboys, and Indians: Deliverance, Conquest, and Liberation Theology Today." *Christianity and Crisis*, 261–65.

CHAPTER 8

Uninterrogated Coloredness and Its Kin

Emilie M. Townes
emilie.m.townes@vanderbilt.edu

. . . invisible things are not necessarily "not there"; . . . a void may be empty, but it is not a vacuum. In addition, certain absences are so stressed, so ornate, so planned, they call attention to themselves; arrest us with intentionality and purpose, like neighborhoods that are defined by the population held away from them. Looking at the scope of American literature, I can't help thinking that the question should have never been "Why am I, an Afro-American, absent from it?" It is not a particularly interesting query anyway. The spectacularly interesting question is "What intellectual feats had to be performed by the author or his critic to erase me from a society seething with my presence, and what effect has that performance had on the work?" What are the strategies of escape from knowledge? Of willful oblivion? . . . Not why. How?
—Morrison 2000, 34–35

orthodox moral discourses ignore the diversities within their (and our) midst

in an ill-timed and increasingly suspect search for an objective viewpoint that can lead us toward the [T]ruth.

often, these inquiries preserve a moral and social universe that has mean-spiritedness at one end of its ontological pole and sycophancy at the other

noblesse oblige often acts as filler and buffer for those trying to maintain or recapture the intellectual and material core of the status quo liberationist discourses of the womanist kind, focus on Morrison's question, "Not why, but how?" as a helpful methodological framework

> to explore how it is that the diversity in our midst is largely ignored in theo-ethical discourses

> or marked as "social sciences" or "politics" as if these astute markers of the human drama are lepers in the house of *theologia*

a second Morrison quote from "Unspeakable Things Unspoken" brings the framework into sharper focus

> For three hundred years black Americans insisted that "race" was no usefully distinguishing factor in human relationships. During those same three centuries every academic discipline, including theology, history, and natural science, insisted "race" was the determining factor in human development. When blacks discovered that they had shaped or become a culturally formed race, and that it had specific and revered difference, suddenly they were told there is no such thing as "race," biological or cultural, that matters and that genuinely intellectual exchange cannot accommodate it . . . It always seemed to me that the people who invented the hierarchy of "race" when it was convenient for them ought not to be the ones to explain it away, now that it does not suit their purposes for it to exist. But there *is* culture and both gender and "race" inform and are informed by it. (2000, 26)

> Morrison notes that the notion of race is still a virtually unspeakable thing

when looking at the ways in which theologies do their work in postmodern societies

> it is important to note that a strong movement within the social sciences to question the efficacy of race as a helpful category to explore our social order

> has been left largely unaddressed by the majority of scholars in the theological disciplines

> we miss, to our methodological peril, to incorporate economics, politics, sex, gender, ethnicity, race, militarism, ageism, and a host of ways we are as deeply theological and not solely social scientific

and more importantly, we fail to see the threads of the intricately knit matrix we are all a part of and even those of us who are liberationists can become single-issue thinkers if we do not keep watch to make sure we have not shut the door to our methodological tool sheds

so, i do not want to move as quickly away as Morrison does from a direct confrontation with race

but propose a different tact in doing so: what i call uninterrogated coloredness

race has been collapsed into this uninterrogated coloredness by academic, economic, ethical, social, theological and political arguments

many of our discussions on race divorce it from the profound impact that color (un)consciousness plays

we focus on darker-skinned peoples almost exclusively

this results in three problems

invites folks of European descent and others to ignore the social construction of whiteness.

allows darker-skinned racial ethnic groups to ignore their internal color caste system.

often opens the door for weird bifurcations of class, race, gender, age and so on.

race is a social construction as well as a cultural production

there are both implicit and explicit costs and benefits to collapsing race into uninterrogated coloredness.

this is usually, if not always, wrapped up in a whirlwind of personal choices and communal power dynamics

genetics tells us that every population is highly variable and whatever external physical signs there may be, genetic features do not absolutely define one population and distinguish it from another

we very rarely stop to think about what is it that we are talking about when we use the word "race."

what images are conjured up

how do those images write themselves large across the academic, theo-ethical, economic, political, and social landscapes?

how do these images situate themselves, if not simply plop themselves down, in the life of religious communities?

we practice a highly selective process of ranking our biological differences in an enormously nuanced and decidedly unscientific system that ignores the fact that color is the least rigorous way to determine race

but we simply cannot ignore, however ill-conceived the notion of race has been and remains—the impact of the ways in which we use coloredness to mark it

in our fascination/fixation on coloredness, we have developed a thoroughgoing yet often unconscious color caste system based on degrees of darkness and lightness[1]

too often our initial response to one another is built from these color cues we have inherited through history, ideology, and memory

race, like gender, class, age, and other manifestations of our humanity, is unstable and decentered

each of these are a complicated and interstructured set of social meanings that are always being transformed by political struggle

making use of the question "how?" helps us recognize the world and our social structures as processes of theological, historical, and social transformation

it enables us to explore the fantastic hegemonic imagination as that which often sparks and fuels supremacist fires

as we have endured a presidential campaign[2] that, to my mind, began far too early, we have seen the destructive effects of latent and not-so-latent racism, sexism, xenophobia, classism, and more—all of which is wrapped in misbegotten jingoistic patriotic drag

each of the major players near the end: clinton, mccain, and obama and the minor players: biden and palin

were flattened, stereotyped, derided, demonized, and at times threatened with death

if liberation theologies are to mean anything, we must address these kinds of moral burps of indigestion

and seek to call for, as we work for in tangible ways; a more just and vibrant social order

in this vein, womanist liberationists can never forget that we stand within a community as active members and participants

the community functions to remind us that we may have lapses within our analysis and critique that demand we reassess our perspectives

but as much as we pay attention to communal accountability, we must also remain vigilant for the forces of hegemony that can and do coopt authentic black life and tempt *us* to replace it with stereotypes and innuendoes that pathologize and victimize segments of the black community

the challenge is how to implement intracommunal accountability without reinscribing hierarchies

answering this question is one of the enduring challenges of womanist thought and to all forms of ethical and theological reflection that focus on black religiosity and African American liberation that is spiritual and social

burned out, bitter people do not help bring in justice very often

so womanist liberationist thought challenges us to dance with twisted hips sometimes[3]

keep the beat

open up our scholarship and give our disciplines the music that challenges threadbare research and mundane, unimaginative theories that reify the status quo

long held notes until the four-part harmony was perfect enough for what we do to reach deep within the academy and boldly outside of it and help create the spaces we know must be there for people to live and have a chance to be whole

so we must put down the temptation to make lists, set quotas, craft exclusive standards of specious excellence, and fight like hell to keep from allowing our work and our lives from becoming monuments of irrelevancy and domination

it is little help, if in our cultural and theo-ethical critiques, we replace the forms of supremacy we know so well

with a postmodern womanist slow drag of annihilation

Notes

1. For a more thorough discussion of this and its particular manifestations within the Black communities of the United States, see my Chapter "'Another Kind of Poetry': Identity and Colorism in Black Life," in Townes (1995, 89–119).
2. The campaigns for the presidential primary and presidential elections of 2008 involving presidential candidates Hilary Clinton, John McCain, Barack Obama, and vice presidential candidates Joe Biden and Sarah Palin.
3. Adapted from Morrison (1987, 89).

Bibliography

Morrison, T. 1987 *Beloved*. New York: Plume/Penguin.

———. 2000. "Unspeakable Things Unspoken: The Afro-American Presence in American Literature." In *The Black Feminist Reader,* ed. Joy James and T. Denean Sharpley-Whiting, 24–56. Malden: Blackwell.

Townes, E. M. 1995. *In a Blaze of Glory: Womanist Spirituality as Social Witness.* Nashville: Abingdon.

PART III

Around the World

CHAPTER 9

Rethinking Liberation: Toward a Canadian Latin@ Theology

Néstor Medina

netto.medina@gmail.com

For Latinas/os in Canada to do theology in a liberationist vein means to develop a multidisciplinary, cross-sectional analysis of the interconnected issues that affect "people of colour" in Canada.[1] It is the intentional weaving of theological reflection with the social sciences, liberal arts, and humanities as necessary requirements for the reflective theological process.[2]

Consistent with the liberation approach, the reality of the people is our point of departure. Here I mention five aspects that ought to be considered in undertaking such an arduous task: highlight the constitution and reality of Latinas/os in Canada; engage in a careful self-reflective analysis of the ideological and sociocultural dynamics at work in these communities; identify the concerns and challenges of Latina/o-Canadians as part of a larger set of concerns in the immigrant communities of Canada; interrogate the myth of Canada as a kind and welcoming country; and recognize that issues of social, political, ethnocultural and racialized injustice, oppression, discrimination, and marginalization are not separate from questions of religious plurality.[3] These five aspects provide the ground rules for developing a Latina/o-Canadian liberation theology.

Latinas/os in Canada

The majority of Latinas/os in Canada[4] have been born outside of its political borders, in their country of origin; the majority of those born in Canada still live with their parents. That is, Latinas/os in Canada are still undergoing the complex and painful process of adapting to a new country, and many are beginning to discover the ambiguity in navigating multiple identity spaces. Latinas/os in Canada are one of the youngest communities when compared to the immigrant and general populations.

One cannot minimize the enormous challenges Latina/o-Canadians confront daily. For most Latinas/os who succeed in migrating to Canada, their arrival marks improved conditions of life, new prosperity, and opportunities. For them, the question of liberation needs to be reconsidered, as to its terms, appropriateness, and desirability in the Canadian context. Latinas/os no longer have to deal with some of the issues for which they left their home countries. If they migrated because of spousal abuse, the laws in Canada make it clear that such behavior is considered criminal. If it is discrimination of any type, be it religion, sexual orientation, or political opinion, Latinas/os feel confident that Canada has taken steps toward preventing such abuses. If it is a question of ethno-cultural discrimination, Canada's facade as the first country to adopt multiculturalism as an official policy eases their concerns. This means that any act of racism is illegal and frowned upon. Finally, if migration was caused because of questions of security, they realize that, generally, Canada is a very safe country, where people are found walking in the streets until the late hours.

Taking this superficial outlook of Canada's sociopolitical and cultural context one could easily assume, as many Latinas/os do, that Canada is a kind of paradise where their children will thrive. Such views are in fact misleading and effectively hide the "dark side" of Canadian official public policy as racist and discriminatory of ethnocultural groups that do not fit the Canadian Eurocentric imaginary.[5] It does not take very long before one realizes that Latinas/os in Canada confront serious obstacles. The initial trauma of being ripped from their countries of origin, family and friends, of learning a new language, and navigating a new system in order to survive contribute to their experience of isolation, depression, and loneliness.[6] Latinas/os quickly learn their education is not recognized in Canada, so they end up working several menial jobs and long hours in order to make ends meet. This is made even more complicated by the dominant culture's pressures and demands for assimilation, and "integration."

Latinas/os are for the most part concentrated in the three large metropolises of Vancouver, Toronto, and Montréal.[7] On average, they are some of the most educated when compared to the total population, but they are among the most underemployed, with the least yearly income index and higher unemployment rates when compared to the total population (Szmulewicz, López, and Ramos 2007). This unique mix of issues leads Latinas/os to be concentrated in "poor neighbourhoods" with precarious living conditions, poor schooling services, and pressures for criminal activity. These social conditions prevent subsequent generations of Latinas/os from having equal opportunities and succeed in this country. The present conditions of poverty, underemployment, and underpayment ensure that certain sectors of the Latina/o community occupy a position of socioeconomic and political disadvantage for years to come.

The Need for a Self-Reflective Analysis of Latinas/os

Not all Latinas/os experience economic disparity and social marginalization in the same way. There are ethnocultural and racialized elements that continue to pervade the population, creating hierarchies of racialized Eurocentric and phenotypical characteristics. Those with lighter skin do all they can to mimic the inherited European notions of racialized superiority. Those of indigenous and African roots continue to be the most discriminated against sectors of the Latina/o communities. Latinas/o from the Central American countries experience greater forms of discrimination even from their fellow Latinas/os. There is the general idea that people from Central America are less educated, ignorant, less "civilized" than their South American, Mexican, and Caribbean counterparts, often connected with the idea that Central Americans are indigenous descendants.

The present system of immigration also feeds into the already existing social class differences. Those who have arrived most recently demonstrate higher levels of institutional education and have succeeded in coming by qualifying through the present "points system." Usually these people migrate because their safety and the safety of their wealth are at risk in their countries of origin. These people usually feel they are entitled to their privileges and wealth and express that those who are poor are so because they are lazy. They establish transnational relations whereby they support conservative governments here and in their countries of origin and their globalizing capitalist policies.[8] These and other elements make it necessary to engage in a self-reflective critical analysis of the present differences that exist between Latina/o groups in which people are discriminated against because of their class, education, and ethnocultural background by members of their own Latina/o community.

The need for a self-reflective analysis includes issues of gender and sexual orientation. Women are still expected to submit to their male counterparts or play a subaltern social role. Many women continue to experience all forms of abuse. Also, the patriarchal culture has to be challenged particularly in its construction of sexual identity. This is especially important when it comes to the patriarchal culture's inability to deal with members of the GLBQTT community. In some of our countries, people are persecuted and even murdered for having a different sexual orientation and this needs to be unmasked and challenged within the Latina/o communities.

Latinas/os and Other Ethnocultural Groups

The disparity and disadvantages that most Latina/o-Canadians experience are not exclusive to them. These issues apply to every ethnocultural group that has arrived within the last 40 years, to the Aboriginals who have suffered since the initial encounter with Europeans, and the African-Canadians and Chinese-Canadians who arrived here before Canada became a nation.[9] In Canada problems of systemic discrimination and structural ethnocultural exclusion and social marginalization are the problem of all people of color. With the exception of Aboriginals, there is a correlation between poverty and recent immigrants.[10] With its Eurocentric imaginary, the present sociopolitical climate denies people of color a fair chance at participating in the construction of the Canadian society.

Canada has a long-standing history of peoples struggling for equality and for the construction of a more democratic society. Canada has its own list of men and women who worked for and adopted the principles of the social gospel, sought to ameliorate the condition of the poor, and who have struggled for justice, equality, fair wages, rights for women, and equal treatment and access to services.[11] One concrete example is the universal health care system ushered in by the Co-operative Commonwealth Foundation, the precursor to the New Democratic Party.

As new ethnocultural groups have made Canada their home, they have discovered that those efforts for emancipation, suffrage, equality, and fairness do not apply to all people in the same way. Canada projects itself to the world as a country where diversity is a core value, a key feature of national identity. Yet, a growing number of studies show that the influence peoples of color can exert over the Canadian society is "tempered by their low incomes, poverty and social exclusion" (Burstein

2007, 42). In other words, multiculturalism isn't working for visibly minoritized groups.[12] People of color need to establish coalitions and engage in struggles with other peoples of color in order to offer alternative ways for reconceiving Canadian culture, identity, and the creation of a more just society.

Interrogating Canada's Official Policy of Multiculturalism

The ubiquitous experience of discrimination and marginalization among immigrants and people of color raises serious questions about Canada's official policy of multiculturalism. The multiethnic European immigrations of the past did not inspire multiculturalism. According to Bannerji, it was only with the presence of people of color that

> diversity came to be seen as really diverse, in spite of the fact that many came from French and English speaking countries, many were Christians, and large numbers had more than a passing acquaintance with cultures of Europe and North America. But as they were not indentured workers, or for the most part not illegals, their presence as workers, taxpayers and electoral constituencies was force to be reckoned with and a problem to be managed. The multicultural policy had to be evolved and put in place for them. (2000, 44)

The policy of multiculturalism impedes the equal social and political participation of other ethnic groups; it prevents many of these people from getting out of poverty because of discrimination in the work place and preserves the Eurocentric imaginary that dominates Canadian society. On one hand, the policy of multiculturalism ensures that people's traditions, cultures, and religions become publicly visible while folklorizing and commodifying them. This bolsters Canada's own presentation to the world as a welcoming country while turning peoples' cultures and religious traditions into exotic elements of consumption within Canada.[13] On the other hand, multiculturalism insists that certain aspects of peoples' cultures and religions remain in the private sphere, effectively neutralizing the social, cultural, and political disruption represented by culturally diverse peoples.

A Canadian liberation theology must expose Canada's own complicit role in the imperial destructive legacy of oppression, discrimination, and erasure of peoples on the basis of ethnocultural origin, and racialized phenotypical characteristics, and specific socioreligious practices. If a liberation theology in Canada is to be different from the liberal optimism of the Social Gospel, it will have to engage in a class analysis of Canada (Cole-Arnal 1998, 148). But a class analysis does not adequately unpack the present interconnected character of systemic injustice based on gender, culture, language, ethnicity, geopolitical origin, and color. It is the job of Latina/o-Canadians to interrogate the present idealized portrait of Canada. Canada's long record of abuses and discrimination against people of color continues to grow even today. The First Nations, Japanese, Chinese, Hungarians, African Canadians,[14] and Accadians[15] are a sample of the growing list of abuses perpetrated against peoples of color that remain unaddressed because of racism and corruption in the present system.[16] Because these issues cut across all of the people of color in Canada, what is needed is the development of "solidarity across racial, ethnic, and national lines in antiracist struggles" (Habell-Pallán 2002, 182).

This leads me to conclude that any liberative notion of theology among Latinas/os in Canada cannot be isolated from people of other cultural groups. Latina/o Canadians together with other Canadians of color must unmask the reality of systemic class discrimination by which Canada only grants entrance to immigrants with considerable financial resources and the brain-drain effect when Canada gives preference to those immigrants who come with high levels of education. Canada does not want refugees! The discrimination is obvious as many people who migrate end up doing something else for work because their education is not recognized in Canada, and because they do not have Canadian experience. In reality, European descendants continue to have access to the best jobs, highest paid positions, and in theology, faculties consistently continue to be White. This shows, that Canada in all levels of government operate with a racialized two tier understanding of citizenship, what Augie Fleras calls "unequal relations" (Fleras and Jean 1992).

In reality, Canada needs immigrants. Canada has the highest percentage of immigrants per capita in the world. By 2026, the high rate of deaths and low rate of births will mean that Canada will depend solely on immigrants to maintain its population (Bollman, Beshiri, and Clemenson 2007, 9). In a very real sense, *salvation* is from the people of color, of which immigrants are a vital part.[17] It is befitting to speak about a preferential option for the immigrant. It is the immigrants who have kept this nation alive since its inception, and it is the people of color who once again will keep it from disappearing.

The official policy of multiculturalism insists that it is possible for people of different cultural and religious backgrounds to live and coexist side by side in "tolerance" of each other. When these people go to the public square, they must leave at home those elements that infringe upon "other people's freedom." For this reason, Bannerji argues that multiculturalism was not put in place for the multiethnic European descendants. While in principle the human person seems to be the highest concern, the principle is dictated from a White-Anglo or White-Francophone perspective that demands that people, while in public, behave the way "white" people do (Bannerji 2000, 43). This leaves the imposed normative sociocultural and political "whiteness" of Canada undisturbed and unchallenged. The Multicultural Act becomes a mechanism of *evitamiento*, it effectively portrays Canada as one of those countries that has dealt with the problem of racism and discrimination by making space for peoples of other cultures and religions, so discussion about racism become taboo and are avoided (Cunin 2003, Chapter 4).

This is the problem that Cármen Aguirre brings out to light as one of the protagonists of her *¿Qué pasa con la raza?*. Skin, comments why she does not fit in the Canadian imaginary:

> I don't feel like I am part of the multicultural mosaic when I'm surrounded by bleeding heart who suffer from amnesia about the history of their country...We are living in Vancouver. A place where white supremacists beat an old Sikh brother to death, where they chase black brothers out of the Ivanhoe with baseball bats, where they beat the crap out of Filipino brothers in Squamish, where everywhere I look I'm portrayed as a fuckin' drug dealer 'cause I'm Latino/a. (Habell-Pallán 2002, 182)

As for academia, whenever one challenges the dominant "white" Eurocentric ethos, one is quickly dismissed as playing identity politics. In theology, students from other groups must learn the inherited dominant European theologians, and only secondarily, one might be able to study one's own religious and theological traditions.

Interreligious Conversations

Challenging Canada's notion of multiculturalism means to challenge the idea that Canada is a secularized country. The Canadian population is profoundly religious. The idea of secularism comes from a dominant Christendom-like perspective that understands the de-Christianization of the country in terms of the growth of secularism. Secularism takes Christianity as the norm and it minimizes the social importance of other religions. People who migrate bring along their religious traditions, practices, and faith expressions, and these are inseparable from the way they conduct themselves in the public sphere. The present reality of ethnocultural diversity introduces an unprecedented religious plurality to the Canadian social fabric. The issue is that the external expressions of these religions are suppressed within the limits of the metropolitan areas preventing other religions from changing and coloring the social spaces of Canadian cities.[18] The issue is far more complicated, but Canada's political and governmental structures continue to operate under a Eurocentric cultural and identity framework colored with predominantly Christian inspired elements.[19]

In the case of Latinas/os, they have also imported their religious affiliations, practices, and expressions of faith. Six of every ten Latinas/os in Canada are Catholics and the remainder are distributed in a variety of religious groups among which evangelicalism and/or Pentecostalism seems to be gaining ground. Thus, a Latina/o-Canadian liberation theological reflection must include careful considerations on religious plurality. It must go beyond ecumenical considerations privileging Christianity and move into interreligious debates that more adequately reflect the present constitution of Latina/o communities and Canada's population.

Transformation of theology

A Latina/o-Canadian reflection means the transformation of the theological task in terms of necessary interdisciplinary engagements. A Latina/o-Canadian liberation theology must be an intercultural, interreligious *teologia en conjunto* whereby Latina/o-Canadians enter into conversation with peoples from other cultures and other religious traditions forming an irreverent cacophony of voices and unique ideas without being stopped by the dominant Eurocentric theology discourses and methods.

This means Latina/o-Canadians and other Canadians need to recover the important role immigrants play in the story of salvation. This demands the development of a hermeneutic of absence by which privilege is given to the groups, peoples, and voices that are silenced and absent from the present configuration of Canadian culture, life, imaginary, and national identity. It also means to unashamedly affirm the unique social public role of religious faith for Latina/o-Canadians. Religious faith helps Latinas/os to cope with the various challenges they face, it also helps them nurture hope for the future as they seek for greater opportunities for their children. This combination of issues is expressed in the way Latinas/os conceive the divine at work. Latina/o faith expressions break with usual patterns of spirituality: Latinas/os violate the established laws and rules of the land and pray to God to not be caught. Latinas/os have been actively praying to God since they left their countries, crossed the borders of other countries without proper "permission," and hoped to arrive to their new country unnoticed.[20] They pray that border patrols will not spot them, or that the coyote will not leave them stranded. Latinas/os pray that they will be able to get fake documents to be able to work, that immigration will not issue a deportation order, or that God will protect them while they stay "illegally" in the country and finally get their papers. It is at the most mundane level in the everyday that Latinas/os display their profound spirituality and connection with the Divine in the forms of prayer, rituals, and vows. So what is at stake is the reconfiguration of theology itself: from the notion of God, salvation, history, to a reconfiguration of creation and the human in light of the ethnocultural mosaic constituting the Canadian population.

Notes

1. I acknowledge that the label "people of colour" is deeply problematic because it places "white" European descendants as the norm of racialized categorization. I use the label as an ethnocultural category.
2. I mean the disruptive reconfiguration of those disciplines to shed light on the condition of peoples of color informing our theological reflection.
3. I use "racialized" to replace the term "race." I agree with the Ontario Human Rights Commission that the category "racialized persons" goes beyond skin color and ethnic background, extending to specific traits and attributes deemed to be "abnormal" and of "less worth."
4. The label "Latin American immigrants" is highly problematic when used as the single category of analysis. See Cáceres (2006, 191).
5. See Bannerji (2000).
6. "Discrimination, lack of language skills, political illiteracy and low SES [socioeconomics] have been identified as some of the major obstacles that Latin American immigrants face when participating in politics" (Ginieniewicz 2006, 40).
7. The number of Latin American immigrants in Canada has almost doubled between 1990 and 2001 to 520,260. Three out of every five Latinas/os reside in Toronto, Montreal, and Vancouver. Toronto is home to 150,000 and Montreal constitutes half of all Latinas/os in Canada (Szmulewicz, López, and Ramos 2007).

8. For example, in 2010 a group of Colombian immigrants expressed their support for president Álvaro Uribe and his Trade Agreement talks with Canada.

9. The first nations and indigenous communities have endured the worst kinds of discrimination and systemic genocide for the longest time (Leddy 1990, 104).

10. See Heisz and McLeod (2004).

11. See McClung (1972), Bland (1973, 1920).

12. See Jiménez (2007).

13. People of other cultural groups are now represented in commercials, ensuring a greater consumption of goods, products, and services by them. See Bird (2004, 185).

14. For example, the children of slaves who settled in Africville, Halifax, around 1940s, were systematically discriminated against and in the 1970s the City expropriated their land. See http://hrsbstaff.ednet.ns.ca/way-mac/African%20Canadian%20Studies/Unit%208.%20Afro-Canada/africville.htm; http://en.wikipedia.org/wiki/Africville,_Nova_Scotia (accessed August 31, 2009).

15. Known as the Great Expulsion (1755–1763), more than 14,000 Acadians (three-quarters of the Acadians in Nova Scotia) were expelled from their territory during the Seven Year's War between England and France.

16. For example, the case of the Somali woman Suaad Hagi Mohamud accused of being an impostor by the Canadian High Commission in Nigeria, who spent three months and one week in prison, until a DNA test proved her identity.

17. For First Nations and Aboriginals, European immigration meant destruction of their way of life, culture, and death. But as "people of colour," they continue to be the object of systemic and structural exclusion and discrimination.

18. Often municipalities stall the construction of sacred buildings because they represent a loss of tax revenue (Germain 2004, 143,145).

19. For example, the 1995 expulsion of high school students in Quebec because they refused to remove their hijab. The Province is working toward making it mandatory in public schools.

20. For fuller discussion of the challenges immigrants experience see Groody and Campese (2008).

Bibliography

Bannerji, H. 2000. *The Dark Side of the Nation: Essays on Multiculturalism, Nationalism and Gender*. Toronto: Canadian Scholar's.

Bird, K. 2004. "Obstacles to Ethnic Minority Representation in Local Government in Canada." *Our Diverse Cities* 1 (Spring): 182–86.

Bland, S. G. 1973. *The New Christianity: The Theology of the Social Gospel*. Toronto: University of Toronto Press.

Bollman, R. D., R. Beshiri, and H. Clemenson. 2007. "Immigrants in Rural Canada." *Our Diverse Cities* 3 (Summer): 9–15.

Burstein, M. 2007. "Promoting the Presence of Visible Minority Groups across Canada." *Our Diverse Cities* 3 (Summer): 42–46.

Cáceres, R. 2006. "A Fragmented Latin American Identity." In *Ruptures, Continuities and Re-Learning: The Political Participation of Latin Americans in Canada*, ed. J. Ginieniewicz and D. Schugurensky, 191–93. Toronto: Transformative Learning Centre, University of Toronto.

Cole-Arnal, O. 1998. *To Set the Captive Free: Liberation Theology in Canada*. Toronto: Between the Lines.

Cunin, E. 2003. *Identidades a flor de piel: Lo "negro" entre apariencias y pertenencias: categorías raciales y mestizaje en Cartagena (Colombia)*. Bogotá: Instituto Colombiano de Antropología e Historia; Universidad de Los Andes.

Fleras, A., and E. Jean. 1992. *Unequal Relations: An Introduction to Race, Ethnic and Aboriginal Dynamics in Canada*. Scarborough: Prentice Hall Canada.

Germain, A. 2004. "Religious Diversity: A Problem for Municipalities." *Our Diverse Cities* 1 (Spring): 143–45.

Ginieniewicz, J. 2006. "Political Participation of Latin Americans in Canada: What Do We Know So Far?" In *Ruptures, continuities and re-learning: The political participation of Latin Americans in Canada*, ed. J. Ginieniewicz and D. Schugurensky, 34–45. Toronto: Transformative Learning Centre, University of Toronto.

Groody, D. G., and G. Campese, eds. 2008. *Promised Land, a Perilous Journey*. Notre Dame: University of Notre Dame.

Habell-Pallán, M. 2002. "'Don't Call Us Hispanic': Popular Latino Theater in Vancouver." In *Latino/a Popular Culture*, ed. M. Habell-Pallán and M. Romero, 174–89. New York: New York University Press.

Heisz, A., and L. McLeod. 2004. "Low Income in Census Metropolitan Areas." *Our Diverse Cities* 1 (Spring): 63–70.

Jiménez, M. 2007. "Do Ethnic Enclaves Impede Integration?" *Globe and Mail*, February 7. http://www.theglobeandmail.com/news/national/do-ethnic-enclaves-impede-integration/article740525/. Accessed October 21, 2009.

Leddy, M. J. 1990. *Say to the Darkness, We Beg to Differ*. Toronto: Lester & Orpen Dennys.

McClung, N. 1972. *In Times Like This*. Toronto: University of Toronto Press.

Szmulewicz, E., M. López, and D. Ramos. 2007. "How is Canada Looking at the Latin-American Immigration: A Backgrounder." Unpublished report. Toronto: Hispanic Development Council.

CHAPTER 10

Key Issues for Liberation Theology Today: Intercultural Gender Theology, Controversial Dialogues on Gender and Theology between Women and Men, and Human Rights

Heike Walz
heike.walz@gmx.ch

The following reflections on key issues of liberation theology today arose when I came back to Germany in 2009 after having lived and taught in Buenos Aires, Argentina, since 2005. I had many questions: What does liberation theology mean for me now, being back in Europe? What did I learn in Latin America? In which way have my perspectives changed?

I wondered if the "original" concept of liberation theology[1] that engages with the transformation of the social reality is still practiced. Or are there social movements and NGOs on the one hand and a kind of "academic liberation theology" on the other?[2] Can this academic liberation theology still be called liberation theology if it is not connected to the historical project of another possible world? Or is it quite "normal" that liberation theology in the twenty-first century has changed its profile? Is it a contemporary approach to liberation theology to adopt the critical analysis of the "world system" and power relations but not necessarily be involved directly in "practical" social engagement? Or has the idea of "organic intellectuals" simply disappeared in the global north? In Latin America, I know intellectuals (especially women) who are also activists.[3]

Liberation theologies have emerged from suffering humanity, having the wounds of the history of colonialism, imperialism, and globalization in mind. The "Third Generation" of liberation theology gives special attention to the experiences of the body, gender issues, desire, and sexualities.[4] Thus, it is possible not only to concentrate on materialistic aspects of *daily life (lo cotidiano)*[5] and *life and survival*[6] but also to analyze critically the socioeconomic and political constructions of society and religion. In this regard I would like to propose three key issues of liberation theology in the twenty-first century that have been part of my area of investigation and engagement: intercultural gender theology, controversial dialogues on gender and theology between women and men, and human rights.

Intercultural Gender Theology

In Latin America, more than ever before, I became aware of European hegemonic thinking. One example is that we have never given up a sort of "Western gender imperialism." I heard this expression in Argentina during discussions about development projects financed by European Mission Agencies and NGOs who work with indigenous communities in Argentina. "The" gender perspective has to be implemented as obligatory in every project in order to receive funding, but white people in Europe and Argentina rarely ask the indigenous people about *their* notion of gender, sexuality, womanhood and manhood, the body, and so on. Usually a Euro-American concept of gender is presupposed. This tendency was heavily criticized in the discussions mentioned above. It was narrated that indigenous communities develop their own contextualized approaches to aspects of daily life we would call "gender issues," but they would not entitle them with the term "gender."[7]

From mission history's beginnings in the sixteenth century[8] Europeans intended to export "civilization," not taking into account that various civilizations do exist. Gender and sexuality norms have always been part of this mission.[9] Even now people in many parts of German society think that women in southern and Oriental parts of the world are more oppressed than in our country. It is rarely examined whether this prejudice fits with reality. Reflections on the criteria used for these judgments are often missing as well.

I also observe that most of the gender approaches in theology in the German-speaking context are influenced by European and North American gender theories. I would like to see more engagement with approaches from non-Western contexts, for example, with Latin American approaches.[10] These approaches are not just a consequence of the "mission" by European and North-American feminists to the South but developments, ideas, and adaptations proper to the indigenous context. Furthermore, gender issues have been developed and "circled around" within international and ecumenical encounters (Walz 2010).

Thus, I argue for an intercultural approach to gender theology.[11] As an example, I want to remember one of the "fore-mothers" of liberation theology in Mexico, Sor Juana Inés de la Cruz (1648–1695), a female scholar, theologian, philosopher, and writer, who developed Latin American aesthetic theology in the seventeenth century.[12] Maria José F. Rosado Nunes, from Brazil, and Beatriz Melano Couch, from Argentina, recognized her as "the first Latin American female theologian" because of her lyrics, theatre, festival, and prose works (de la Cruz 1995) rich in theological content and reflection.[13] I appreciate particularly her contributions to intercultural reflection, because she addresses the power conflicts between the indigenous, black, mixed,[14] and European groups in Mexico. She recognized the ethnic-cultural hybrid mixture of the society in her time (Gonzalez 2007, 233). Sor Juana dignified the religions of the indigenous and black people of her time, for example, in her theatre work *El Divino Narciso*. Some scholars named her "feminist" or "proto-feminist" because of her gender consciousness. She recognized that the ethnic and cultural background of the population intersects with gender issues. Sor Juana defended the position that women and men do have equal intellectual capacities so that girls and women should also receive schooling and education (Gonzales 2003, 111–13). Interestingly she considered aesthetic language as most adequate for theology (Gonzalez 2003, 57–91, 137–38). Hence, in her works she combines beauty, justice, and truth so that liberation theology can draw inspiration from her today, as Michelle Gonzalez proposes (2003, xii).

With respect to such interesting and critical voices from Latin America there is a great challenge for me in Europe, especially as a theologian engaged with gender and liberation theology: How can we resist Euro-American "gender imperialism"? How can we emphasize the contributions of indigenous and mixed communities and female and male intellectuals in Latin America? How do we deal with the different forms of "cosmo-vision" of indigenous people—especially the wisdom that has been rejected and oppressed by Eurocentric thinking until now?

Gender Dialogues between Women and Men and Crosswise

My second suggestion is situated on a methodological level as well. Gender issues and sexualities in theology need not only be discussed in dialogue settings between women and men but also "crosswise"[15] in the sense of a broad dialogue on bodies, genders, and sexualities in theology. In 2004, I cofounded the "Network of Gendered Theology" (NGT)[16] together with female and male colleagues. It aims at initiating such dialogues between women and men theologians (and all people who consider themselves beyond the dual sex system) about gender and theology.[17]

Feminist theologians, male theologians doing "critical men's studies on religion,"[18] lesbian and gay theologians, and queer theologians take part in this project. The participants are from Germany, Austria, and Switzerland; some of them live in the United States. The situation in German-speaking countries is as follows: feminists, critical men, gay, lesbian, and queer theologians doing theology and working on religion have been working out their ideas by discussing them in specialized circles. In most cases these circles do not have much communication and interaction with each other. Their approaches have been more or less separated and sidelined by mainline theology.

It is necessary to bring these scholars and theologians engaged in church praxis in dialogue with each other. The aim is to avoid "hermetically sealed" islands that tend to repeat the same discourses without addressing "blind spots," taboos, and controversial topics. Furthermore, we have observed that some theologians do no longer identify themselves exclusively in one circle of debate (for example, feminist or gay) but are rather engaged crosswise in various circles.[19] Thus, I argue for controversial and constructive dialogues that address the conflict points between the "islands," the controversial issues with mainstream theology, and the debates with theories in gender studies. Let me give six more reasons for these crosswise gender dialogues in theology.[20]

First, it is illuminative when *women and men* from different churches, academic, and praxis contexts dialogue with each other about their—different, similar, and opposed—experiences and concepts of sex, gender identity, and sexuality (to put it in a threefold way, like Judith Butler [2004] does). This is important in order to address the complexity and ambiguity of gender violence; gendered division of labor; gendered income gaps; new forms of globalized hegemonic masculinity that affect women as well; motherhood, fatherhood, and parenthood; poverty; international women trafficking; violence against lesbian, gay, bisexual, transvestite, transsexual (LGBTT); child abuse; and of course theological questions of masculinized constructions of the divine, desexualized theologies, body theology, etcetera.

The second argument is that the *different theoretical approaches* to gender and queer theory can be discussed openly and controversially. Some theologians believe in biological differences between women and men,[21] others engage with poststructuralist deconstruction of gender in queer theory.[22] Some might engage with postcolonial theories and theologies,[23] others with recent theories of the intersection of gender and diversity.[24]

Third, the aim is to bridge the *gap between academic theology and church praxis,* which has not only been criticized by feminist theologians but has also been addressed by critical men's studies in religion and likewise by church members and students of theology. The fourth argument is that dialogues between *cultural gender studies and theology* are necessary. In German-speaking contexts, theology and religious studies in university programs of gender studies are absent.

The fifth argument is that gender dialogues crosswise are a contribution to intercultural theology in *inter-denominational and ecumenical perspectives,* and they engage with contextual and planetary questions from the *global South.*

My last point is that gender issues, gender, and sexual politics must be addressed in *strategic alliances* between women and men, and also between the different islands, instead of opposing and combating women's issues, men's issues, and LGBTT. The aim is to highlight that violent gender structures intersect. This is not easy. We have experienced that everybody feels more connected to his or her own suffering and concerns. Issues regarding the Other are often overlooked, even within gender engaged circles. The objective should be to stop pitting one's own suffering and analysis against the suffering and analysis of the Other, which means to develop solidarity. Theologically speaking: What do I have in common with my sisters' theological concerns of transsexuals, if I am a heterosexual believing in biological differences of humanity?

Interestingly almost all gender theologians do share *one* common point. Most of the theologians have been influenced by Latin American liberation theology and try to elaborate a liberationist theology from their perspective and their context of gender engagement, such as feminist, gay, lesbian, queer theology, post-Holocaust theology, postcolonial theology, postmodern theology, indigenous theology, intercultural theology, migration theology, etcetera. There is also a second agreement, originally coming from the tradition of liberation theology: participants of the network do theology beginning with a reflection on their daily life experiences, church, and university praxis or engagement in the society.

These *face-to-face dialogues* or *written dialogues* are an innovative project for the future of liberation theology, because different and controversial opinions and perspectives are openly discussed and the horizon is widened. Gender issues are very complex and often ambiguous and contradictory, so that it is no longer sufficient to concentrate exclusively on women's experience, just to give an example. If one works on "motherhood" in heterosexual and homosexual relationships, unconsciously a sort of conception of "fatherhood" is in mind, but rarely it is expressed or reflected. In dialogue the interdependence of female and male constructions are getting more visible. Politically controversial questions of authority can be addressed: Who is authorized to talk about giving birth and care of children?[25]

In recent years we have discussed questions related to the body: How far can the deconstruction of the body go, without disregarding basic material concerns and embodied realities? We try to learn to live with different approaches, to respect them, and to learn from these differences. One becomes aware of the limits of one's own perspective. A sort of "culture of dialogue" has developed. We also detect that the setting of crosswise gender dialogues on theology attracts young theologians doing research work on gender issues in theology. As we are critical of rigid standpoints, they feel free to discuss their perspectives. Many of them reject the separation of "feminists" and "critical men"; they want to do gender theology together. The network offers such a space also for mentorship by other theologians.

My standpoint is a combination of the deconstruction of gender imaginations, gender, and sexuality norms with the liberation theological focus on "material questions": Are basic needs and survival of the marginalized part of theology? Is sexuality part of theology, as Marcella Althaus-Reid asked critically (2000, 2006). Does the theological perspective and reflection begin from the periphery? I proclaim a sort of deconstructive liberation theology, which takes into account the question of the cross: Who is suffering? Who is missing and set apart? But again: this is only *one* position in the midst of the crosswise dialogues with others.

Human Rights as a Key for Liberation Theology

Maybe it is surprising that the third key issue is human rights. I understand human rights to be a perspective of the victims of structural violence. During my time in Argentina the question of human rights was more and more put on the top of the agenda, especially since 2003, and even in governmental politics. Since the last dictatorship (1976–1983) human rights movements, such as the Mothers and Grandmothers of the Plaza de Mayo, have permanently challenged the society to put an end to impunity for the crimes against humanity during the last dictatorship.[26] Theologically it seems to be like the "pertinacity of resurrection," as Nancy Bedford (2008) titled her book on feminist theology.

Therefore, my attention has been directed toward theological reflections of human rights since then. Even if the human rights charter has been criticized as a Western cultural product or even a Christian one, Argentine human rights organizations have utilized and adopted human rights as an instrument of resistance in Argentina. Human rights even serve as a matrix of analysis of society, as Argentine sociologist Fortunato Mallimaci (2007) puts it. Human rights also serve as a working tool to criticize the lack of the "right to decide" with respect to women's rights, reproductive rights and sexual rights, and issues of gender violence, such as male violence against women and children, and violence against LGBTT. Thus, they serve as a tool to fight for the rights of the lesbian, gay, bi- and transsexual, or transvestite people.

How do liberation theology and human rights relate to each other?[27] Can human rights serve as a key for the articulation of liberation theology in the twenty-first century? During the last years I have observed a tension in Argentina. Military dictatorships were the context of the birth of liberation theology, but although authoritative regimes ended more than 25 years ago, people in Argentina stress that in times of a so-called democratic system forms of systematic oppression of a great part of the population continue every day. The percentage of the poor population is increasing.[28]

This is one reason why a large number of my colleagues in Argentina continue to articulate liberation theology as a fundamental critique of the economic system of neoliberalism.[29] Against that, theologians in the global North (and sometimes also in the global South) state that liberation theology has to be permanently rearticulated, especially now as the situation is much more complicated.

I am situated in between, because I think there is a need to rearticulate liberation theological thinking continuously, but at the same time it is very clear that the gap between the marginalized and the rich is getting worse. There is no better access to social rights though the population is living in a democratic system. My suggestion is that human rights could serve as a tool to articulate these questions: poverty is a human rights question; the same applies not only to gender violence, women's rights, reproductive and sexual rights but also to cultural rights of indigenous people and the rights of the immigrants. The question is, how the Euro-American concept of human rights has already been revised, adopted, and changed by Latin American perspectives and also by the critical perspective and methodology of liberation theology.

These are my three fountains to nourish gendered liberation theology in the twenty-first century: intercultural gender approaches, gender dialogues on theology crosswise, and the question of human rights. The three aspects are related with each other, seeking for survival of the marginalized and fight for respectful and attentive approaches toward the Other. I have just opened up the debate here, many aspects have to be deepened and reflected more profoundly in future.

Notes

1. See Gutiérrez (1988).
2. This issue was discussed in the first "World Forum of Liberation Theology" in Porto Alegre, 2005, see Althaus-Reid, Petrella, and Susin (2007).
3. See Gutiérrez (2011).
4. See Althaus-Reid (2006).
5. See Gebara (2002, 123).
6. See Tamez (2001).
7. I was involved in such discussions during the "Interconfessional Encounter of Missionaries working with Indigenous People in the Chaco" addressing the Bicentenary of the Argentine Nation, September, 25–27, 2009, in Sáenz Peña in Argentina.
8. See Huber and Lutkehaus (1999).
9. See the book mostly written from the point of view of women theologians from the global South: Lienemann-Perrin, Joye, and Longkumer (2012). My contribution is about the impact of women missionaries from Germany and Switzerland.
10. See Marcos (2006) and her contribution in this book.
11. See Aquino (2007) and Kim (2011).
12. Gonzalez (2003).
13. See Rosado (1996) and Melano (2001).
14. *Criollas/os, mestizo/as, mulata/os,* and *indigenous* people.
15. In German we use the word *querbeet*, which alludes to "queer" and to the "field." We want to express that the dialogues take place with respect to all gender dimensions, crossing the whole field of gender, such as the body, gender identities, desires, and sexualities; see Walz and Plüss (2008).
16. With Dr. Tania Oldenhage, Christoph Walser, Sabine Scheuter, and Andreas Borter; see www.netzwerk-ngt.org, accessed March 3,2012.

17. The first publication of the dialogues of the Network is Walz and Plüss (2008).
18. Björn Krondorfer prefers this expression; see Krondorfer (2009).
19. See Althaus-Reid and Isherwood (2007).
20. See Walz (2008, 2011).
21. See Walser, Prömper, and Rödiger (2008).
22. See Fischer and Hess (2008) and Schippert, Söderblom, and Brinkschröder (2008).
23. See Moore and Rivera (2010).
24. See Winkler and Degele (2009) and Walgenbach et al. (2007).
25. See Oldenhage et al. (2008).
26. See Walz (2009).
27. My current investigation is about Human Rights and Theology in Latin America, with Argentina as a case study.
28. Official data from 2011 states 32 percent, whereas the Roman Catholic Church states 34.9 percent. Other calculations of poverty include figures of 44 percent or even 50 percent, which is alarming; see http://discepolin.blogspot.com/2011/04/argentina-2011-sigue-progresando-la.html (accessed March 3, 2012).
29. See Krüger (2006).

Bibliography

Althaus-Reid, M. 2000. *Indecent Theology. Theological Perversions in Sex, Gender and Politics.* New York: Routledge.

———, ed. 2006. *Liberation Theology and Sexuality.* Aldershot: Ashgate.

Althaus-Reid, M., and Isherwood, L., eds. 2007. *Controversies in Feminist Theologies.* London: SCM.

Althaus-Reid, M., Petrella, I., and Susin, L. C., eds. 2007. *Another Possible World.* Reclaiming Liberation Theology Series. London: SCM.

Aquino, M. P., ed. 2007. *Feminist Intercultural Theology. Latina Explorations for a Just World* Maryknoll: Orbis Books.

Bedford, N. E. 2008. *La porfía de la resurrección. Ensayos desde el feminismo teológico latinoamericano.* Buenos Aires: Ediciones Kairos.

Butler, J. 2004. *Undoing Gender.* New York: Routledge.

de la Cruz, J. I. 1995. *Obras completas de Sor Juana Inés de la Cruz,* 4 vols., ed. Alfonso Méndez Plancarte and Alberto Salcede. México: Instituto Mexiquense de Cultura.

Fischer, M., and Hess, R. 2008. "Theologische Männerforschung versus theologische GeschlechterDeKonstruktion. Ein Wortwechsel." In *Theologie und Geschlecht. Dialoge querbeet,* ed. Heike Walz and David Plüss, 158–91. Münster: LIT.

Gebara, I. 2002. *Out of the Depths. Women's Experience of Evil and Salvation.* Minneapolis: Fortress.

Gonzalez, M. A. 2003. *Beauty and Justice in the Americas.* Maryknoll: Orbis Books.

————. 2007. "Sor Juana Inés de la Cruz (1651–1695)." In *Empire and the Christian Tradition*, ed. Kwok Pui-lan, Don Compier and Jörg Rieger, 229–42. Minneapolis: Fortress.

Gutiérrez, G. 1988. *Liberation Theology: History, Politics, and Salvation*, 15th Anniversary Edition. Maryknoll: Orbis Books.

Gutiérrez, M. A., ed. 2011. *Voces polifónicas. Itinerarios de los géneros y las sexualidades*. Buenos Aires: Ediciones Godot.

Huber, M. T., and N. C. Lutkehaus, eds. 1999. *Gendered Missions. Women and Men in Missionary Practice and Discourse*. Ann Arbor: University of Michigan Press.

Kim, K. 2011. "Gender Issues in Intercultural Theology." In *Intercultural Theology. Approaches and Themes*, ed. Mark Cartledge and David Cheetham, 75–92. London: SCM.

Krondorfer, B. 2009. *Men and Masculinities in Christianity and Judaism. A Critical Reader*. London: SCM.

Krüger, R., ed. 2006. *Vida plena para toda la creación. Iglesia, globalización neoliberal y justicia económica*. Buenos Aires: AIRPRAL.

Lienemann-Perrin, C., A. S. Joye, and A. Longkumer, eds. 2012. *Putting Names with Faces: Women's Impact on Mission*. Nashville: Abingdon.

Mallimaci, F. 2007. "Los derechos humanos y la ciudadanía como matriz de análisis de nuestra sociedad." In *Población y bienestar en Argentina del primero al segundo centenario. Una historia social del Siglo XX*, vol. 1, ed. Susana Torrado, 1–22. Buenos Aires: EDHASA.

Marcos, S. 2006. *Taken from the Lips. Gender and Eros in Mesoamerican Religions*. Leiden: Brill.

Melano, B. C. 2001. "Sor Juana Inés de la Cruz. Primer mujer teóloga de América." In *Juntando hilos de teología feminista*, ed. María Josê F. Nunes Rosado and Beatriz Couch Melano, 57–75. Buenos Aires: Católicas por el Derecho a Decidir.

Moore, S. D., and M. Rivera, eds. 2010. *Planetary Loves: Spivak, Postcoloniality, and Theology*. New York: Fordham University Press.

Oldenhage, T., S. Scheuter, A. Borter, and D. Plüss. 2008. "Mutter/Vater durch Geburt." In *Theologie und Geschlecht. Dialoge querbeet*, ed. Heike Walz and David Plüss, 38–56. Berlin: LIT Verlag.

Rosado, M. J. F. N. 1996. "La voz de las mujeres en la teología Latinoamericana." *Concilium* 262, 13–28.

Schippert, C., K. Söderblom, and M. Brinkschröder. 2008. "Queer Theorie. Ein Gespräch zwischen Theorie und Praxis." In *Theologie und Geschlecht. Dialoge querbeet*, ed. Heike Walz and David Plüss, 103–33. Berlin: LIT Verlag.

Sor Juana Inés de la Cruz, Redondillas. Hombres necios que acusáis a la mujer, sin razón, sin ver que sois la ocasión de lo mismo que culpáis. http://www.analitica.com/Bitblio/juana_ines/hombres_necios.asp. Accessed March 3, 2012.

Tamez, E. 2001. *Da hasste ich das Leben. Eine Lektüre des Buches Kohelet*. Luzern: Edition Exodus.

Walgenbach, K., G. Dietze, A. Hornscheidt, and K. Palm. 2007. *Gender als inter-dependente Kategorie. Neue Perspektiven auf Intersektionalität, Diversität und Heterognität.* Opladen: Barbara Budrich.

Walser, C., H. Prömper, and K. Rödiger. 2008. "Männliche Megalomanie— symbolisch dekonstruiert." In *Theologie und Geschlecht. Dialoge querbeet,* ed. Heike Walz and David Plüss, 136–57. Berlin: LIT Verlag.

Walz, H. 2008. "Blinde Flecken. Warum es theologische Geschlechterdialoge querbeet braucht." In *Theologie und Geschlecht. Dialoge querbeet,* ed. Heike Walz and David Plüss, 10–36. Münster: LIT.

———. 2009. "*Madres* Appear on the Public *Plaza de Mayo.* Towards Human Rights as a Key for a Public Theology that Carries on the Liberation Heritage." *International Journal of Public Theology* 3:2, 164–86.

———. 2010. "Interkulturelle Theologie und Geschlecht. Herausforderungen für Europa am Beispiel lateinamerikanischer Theologinnen." *BThZ* 27:1, 107–32.

———. 2011. "Ökumenische Dialoge zu Geschlechterbewusster Theologie." *Junge Kirche* 72:4, 48–50.

Walz, H., and D. Plüss, eds. 2008. *Theologie und Geschlecht. Dialoge querbeet.* Münster: LIT.

Winkler, G., and N. Degele. 2009. *Intersektionalität. Zur Analyse sozialer Ungleichheiten.* Bielefeld: Transcript.

CHAPTER 11

The Revolution in the Arab World. Liberation: The Promise and the Illusion; A Palestinian Christian Perspective

Mitri Raheb
diyar@diyar.ps

It is not by chance that I am not using in the title the much used phrase "The Arab Spring," first used in 2005 by the Lebanese thinker of Palestinian origin Samir Kassir (2005,1). I am not using it because it brings with it a positive connotation and qualification that I cannot take as a given. Rather I would like to look at what is happening in the Arab world today only in a dialectical way: this Arab revolution, I firmly believe is open ended and carries with it both a promise of liberation and an illusion of a new era at the same time.

To know where we stand today, we need to see where we come from, hoping that this will help us understand where we are heading. If we look back at the history of the Middle East in the last 100 years, we see that there were six decisive moments that shaped this history in the last half century in our region and that led to this moment.

Where Do We Come From?

1. One cannot understand what is happening today in the Middle East unless we go back to the First World War. With the defeat of the German Turkish alliance, the Ottoman Empire was dissolved. The Arabs who were given the promise of national liberation by the British came to see that those promises were nothing but lip

service. Instead, new countries with new boundaries were created in the Fertile Crescent and were put under the mandate of the victorious powers of England and France, and a new promise was given instead by Lord Balfour to create a National Homeland for the Jewish people in Palestine. This was the only promise fulfilled. So the promises around First World War ended as one of the greatest illusions in history.

2. We have to remember that all of these leaders being ousted from the Middle East today came to power through national revolutions. They were the revolutionaries 40 years ago. They brought with them at that time the promise of independence from the "Colonial West"; they brought with them the promise of unity of the Arab world; the promise of socialism that the ordinary person would have a better life. This was true for Nasser Ghadafi and Mubarak after him, Borkeba who preceded Bin Ali in Tunisia, Assad the father. So the national revolutions were the second decisive moment.

3. The third decisive moment was in 1967 when all of these leaders were defeated by Israel. This moment was the first time when the people in the Arab world were faced with the fact that the revolution was an illusion. Great revolutions ended up in humiliating defeat, and this sense of being defeated has shaped the last 40 years in the Arab world.

4. The fourth decisive moment came shortly after the 1967 war: it was the discovery of oil as a political weapon and the emerging of the so-called Petro-Dollar. For the first time in the history of our region the center of gravity moved from the so-called Fertile Crescent to the Arab Peninsula and to the Gulf region. The influence of countries such as Saudi Arabia or Qatar became slowly but surely very visible and a desert culture started invading the landscape of the Middle East.

5. The fifth decisive moment came in 1979 when another revolution, this time an Islamic one, took place. This Islamic revolution came to throw away a dictator, the "Shah." So basically, Iran had their current revolution 30 years ago, when a dictator was removed and the promise of a divine state became loud.

6. And last but not least, the sixth decisive moment in the Middle East came in 1982. Here, I do not mean the Lebanon war. I am talking about another revolution. This revolution happened under the radar, but for me this might be the most important revolution. The year 1982 was the year of the electronic revolution when

the world moved away from typewriters to computers. This revolution was not about typing; this revolution changed the whole economy worldwide, and it changed the whole way of education. This revolution was the only revolution that did not make a stop in the Arab world; it bypassed our region. In the United Nations "Arab Human Development Report (2003)," one can see how the development in the Arab world up until 1982 was parallel with the rest of the world. However, starting in 1982, the Arab world began sliding downward because the governments did not recognize the importance of this revolution and so they missed the future.

Thus, that is where we came from 100 years ago. However, during these 100 years a new generation was born. The old generation "who left Egypt" through all of these revolutions "died in the desert" and was not able to see "the Promised Land." This new generation looked around and what did they see?

Where Are We Now?

1. The new Arab generation did not see anything left from those national revolutions, nothing but a security state that makes their life miserable. The other thing that this generation saw was that all of the nation states were run as private businesses: power was handed over from father to son even in the most socialist oriented countries; the wife of "X" controlled 70 percent of the economy; the brother of "Y" ran a good portion of the state business and so on. This new generation "born in the desert" became totally disillusioned. One month before the whole revolution started, we conducted a study on the "Cultural Practices of the Palestinian Youth," and our findings were that only 18 percent of the young people in Palestine were connected to a political party. The majority did not even want to hear the word politics; they were disillusioned.

2. This new generation born in the desert heard throughout their life that Israel was the enemy, and yet they felt that the 1967 defeat is continuing. I mean the rhetoric was that all the Arab countries were working hard to free Palestine, but these young people saw the second intifada; they watched the war on Gaza, and they felt humiliated. And it is not easy to feel, as young people, humiliated.

3. This new generation born in the desert opened their eyes to find a polarized society. They turned on the television stations and all what they saw were either clergy men preaching or belly dancers and nothing in between. It is very tough to live in such a polarized society, where you do not have anything in the middle. It is very interesting that in the study Diyar did on "Cultural Practices of the Palestinian Youth," there was a question about religion. The answers to this question were polarized. The young people in Palestine were either totally for religion or totally against religion. But what is in common among all of the young people of this new generation was that they do not have a problem in "worshiping the golden calf" or what we call today consumerism. The one event at our center that attracted the biggest number of young people was an Egyptian film called "Omar wa Salma," starring the young Egyptian actor Tamer Hosni, who is like the superstar of the young people in the Arab world. This film was the only event where we had 2,200 young people pouring into the streets and closing the old city because they wanted to see it. I said to myself that I have to see what this film is all about! It was about the new Arab consumer society. The film was showing the young people, the cars, mobiles, iPads, girls and boys in open relationships, and so on...what they are dreaming of but do not have: the promise of the illusion.

4. This new generation born in the desert was 25 percent unemployed. This is a generation born in the desert that was brought up with television satellite dishes on the top of their homes with 1000+ channels; this is a generation that spends three hours a day on average on Facebook, as it has its morning devotion with Facebook and before it goes to bed a good night kiss is given to the social networking website. Facebook is their liturgy, and they take it much more seriously than Christians reading their Bible. And what this generation sees through this 1000+ television channels and through Facebook raises their expectations higher and higher; they see all of these endless possibilities and they want to tap into it.

Born in the desert, the road to the Promised Land for this new generation was possible only virtually. The feeling became so strong among these young people that they are "stuck in the desert": the desert is very rough and the heat is very high, and so things started to boil. There was a silent people's revolution going on because the frustration of the young people was accumulating, and all what it needed was just someone to put it on fire, which a young man in Tunisia did. After him, the Middle East started shaking. A Tsunami swept through the Arab world, starting in Tunisia, Egypt, Libya, Yemen, Bahrain, Syria, Jordan, Morocco, and maybe others to follow, with the exception of Palestine. For the first time, we had the luxury in Palestine not to be on television screens but to sit and watch. For a change, this was really good. We were able at least to catch our breath. But the changes in the Arab world will have their impact on Palestine. Right now it is forcing Fatah and Hamas to reposition themselves waiting for the dust of the revolution to clear before they will take a more stable position.

The Liberation: A Promise and/or an Illusion?

The revolutions in the Middle East are both a promise and an illusion; thus, a dialectical relationship.

The promise: we see a new era starting in the Middle East, after which the region will not be the same anymore. And yet, we have the same people and the same infrastructure. There is a new hope that one feels for the first time in 40 years in the Middle East. It is very compatible with Obama's "Yes We Can," for these young people in Middle East are saying just that. This is the promise. However, the illusion is this: it is easier said than done because it still needs hard work. We see how Obama's promises are fading away. Are the young people in the Arab world ready for a long and thorny process?

The promise: it is the young people who are not politicized who are pouring into the streets as in the 1960s in Europe. Yet the illusion: without the military, nothing would have been possible. The military in Egypt, who appeared to behave "neutrally," was in favor of change; it is the Western military strikes in Libya that made the change, and it is the military in Syria that is keeping leaders there in power.

We have the promise of new emerging political parties. We watched the elections in Tunisia with several parties competing. Such promise is great for this is what we needed: an alternative to the ruling parties on the one hand and to the Islamists in opposition on the other. Yet, the illusion is that the Islamists are the most organized so far. Perhaps the most important and decisive question in the Middle East today is not whether we are entering a new Islamic era. But rather what kind of one? Which Islamic model is going to prevail? The Saudi, the Turkish, the one in Dubai, or any other? Most probably several Islamic models will compete with each other over who is more authentic and who is more successful.

It seems to me that a kind of a neoconservative Islam is on the horizon. It is religiously conservative but very much consumer oriented and thus economically neoliberal, and it can satisfy to some extent some "needs" of the people of the Middle East and this would fit very well with Western interests with a consumer market of 350 million Arab people.

The Middle East seems to be undergoing a radical change. Nevertheless, the actual change is still limited.

However, we are experiencing a new regrouping between those countries who have a monarchy and oil on the one hand and those who are experiencing revolutions but have only scarce resources on the other; between those who can satisfy the consumer needs of their people but not necessarily their rights and those who might be able to satisfy the rights of their people but not their needs. This is a scary situation.

Besides, there is a real danger right now to see the Middle East being dismantled and "Balkanized": Sudan was divided into two; Iraq might be divided by three; Lebanon continues to be turned into two like Palestine (West Bank versus Gaza), and we do not know how many "Libyas" and "Yemens" will come out of this war. Thus, what we might be witnessing is the whole Middle East becoming fractured.

The region might be split also between Shiites and Sunni Muslims. Such a scenario might push the region into new wave of militarization that would exploit the resources of the region and that would only benefit the warlords in the region and the weapons trade.

The promise: for the first time in the Arab world we have a revolution that is so peaceful. What happened in Tunisia and in Egypt was very much like what happened in Leipzig in Germany, when candles brought down the walls. Yet, in Libya, Syria, and maybe other countries, it is very bloody. To conclude this point, the revolution should not be underestimated, but at the same time, it should not also be overestimated. As someone who believes more in process than in revolution, the promise of this revolution can only be if it is to be at the beginning of the process; the revolution is just the beginning, and the process is yet to deliver. The work is not behind us, it has just started.

Toward a Public Theology of Liberation

It is very difficult to predict where we are heading; it is perhaps easier to say where we should be heading. For the promise to yield fruit, we need to remember where we came from and what still needs to be done. One of the most crucial steps that is urgent is to develop a public theology of liberation for the Arab world today. There are seven components for such a theology:

1. Liberation is what the Arab peoples are longing for. Liberation is a central theme in the Bible. Liberation from oppression as well as liberation from the religious Laws. In this sense theologians in the Arab world have a very unique calling to articulate and help liberate their peoples from dictatorships and oppressive regimes as well as making sure that the new Islamist parties will not oppress peoples with new religious laws that would violate human rights.

2. For the liberation to be true, we need a new legislation and modern constitutions. When Moses was able to get rid of Pharaoh, what came immediately after going through the Red Sea? The law—the Ten Commandments. A new constitution was needed, and everyone was under the rule of law, including Moses. This is why Moses was not able to enter the Promised Land, because he was also under the law; it is called accountability today.

3. For the liberation to yield fruit, the region has to move from a one-party system that has been the norm in the Arab world into a multiparty system where the Islamists are also included. There are a few very important questions that need to be dealt with in this regard. One of them is the relationship between religion and state. Also, whatever the solution is or the formula, there is no way but through a civil society. In fact, if we wonder why the revolution in Egypt was so peaceful compared with Syria, the answer is that there is a strong civil society in Egypt while there is almost no civil society in Syria. And if we ask why the *annahda* Islamic party in Tunisia is more progressive than the one in Libya, the answer is in the civil society. Therefore, the work that was carried out through the many nongovernmental organizations over the last 20 years was important although people were not able to see it at that time.

4. The Arab world that is threatening to balkanize and fragment needs a new and inclusive vision. Jerusalem at Pentecost could function here as the paradigm, where you have different identities represented by the different languages, yet communication was possible through the spirit. The Arab world is in need for a new spirit that is based on the notion of citizenship. Citizenship is important because it provides unity throughout all the diversities we have in the Middle East, including religious, ethnic, national, and so on.

5. For the liberation to bring fruit, we need to solve the Palestinian question. Without solving this conflict there will be no possibility for the Middle East to focus on development. We cannot focus on development, on economy, and on the future unless this conflict is set aside once and for all; otherwise, it will pull the whole region down again. When it came to Palestine, theology was unfortunately part of the problem most of the time rather than part of the solution. This is true not only for Christian Zionist theology but also for a liberal theology of the Judeo-Christian dialogue that left the occupation of Palestine under the radar of dialogue. Liberation of the Palestinian Arab people from the Israeli occupation and the liberation of the Arab nations from dictatorship are the two sides of the same coin.

6. Liberation has to meet the expectations of the young people and future generation. What are their expectations? They need education: with an illiteracy rate of 35.6 percent in the Arab world (compared to 18 percent globally). They need jobs in a region with the world's lowest employment rate and where in the coming ten years over 50 million new jobs need to be created. Who can do that? They want a job; they want space to move freely, to be able to express themselves without fearing the security state; they want to have life and to have it abundantly. All of this is not possible without a new unifying vision for the region at large and for each country separately. The people of the Middle East have to take responsibility for building their future together.

7. We are in urgent need for a prophetic theology if the liberation is to be a real liberation and not an illusion. And by the way, no one is a spectator, we are all actors: the Arab people are actors, they have proven that; the governments in the Middle East are actors so what they do is important; the United States is an actor; Europe is an actor; and Turkey, Iran, and Israel are actors. However, we feel there are conflicting interests between the values the actors say they believe in—such as democracy, human rights, development, and so on—and the "real politics" of oil, weapon trades, and markets. The interests of the Western countries in oil, the support they have been giving over decades to all the dictators as long as they are in power, and the sudden turn against them once they start to tremble are just signs of this real politics of oil, weapon, and markets and has little to do with human rights or democracy. Prophetic theology has to point to these double standards and this inconsistency between what countries preach

and what they end up doing. Prophetic theology should make sure that the Hypocrisy of these countries is uncovered and dealt with.

So when we look at the revolutions, we continue to be torn between the promise and the illusion. Yet the only option we have is to assume responsibility, to develop a Public Theology of liberation for the Arab world, and to become even more active toward a real process of change from within.

Bibliography

Kassir, S. 2005. "The Arab Spring." *Annahar Newspaper*, March 4, 1.

CHAPTER 12

Liberation Theology and Indigenous People

Wati Longchar
wlongchar@gmail.com

The development of two-thirds world contextual local theologies is a part of the larger movement for liberation and selfhood. Though contextualization of theology has been the way of doing theology throughout the history of Christian thought, the recent contextual theologies in the two-thirds world, such as dalit theology, minjung theology, feminist theology, and others, significantly differ in their methodology, approach, focus, and content from dominant theological paradigms. Despite the primary focus and goal of these theologies being liberation, their approaches to liberation are different. For example, feminist/womanist theology reflects the struggle of women in the context of their experience of oppression and marginalization in male dominated structures and a major focus is on women's liberation. Black theology reflects "Black experience" and the struggle of Black people. Minjung theology is a product of the struggle of the Korean people against the dictatorial regime exercised particularly in the 1970s. Dalit theology's main focus is to dismantle the oppressive caste structure and liberate the dalit from caste discrimination. Similarly, the methodology and perspective of indigenous theology also differs from other contextual or dominant theologies. Therefore, this essay attempts to highlight the distinctiveness of indigenous theology to widen the perspective of liberation theology.

Indigenous People's Context Demands Collective Resistance for Justice

Indigenous peoples constitute about 5 to 8 percent of the world population. They are the first people, the original settlers of the land who gave names to their mountains, rivers, rocks, and others. Naming of a child is the right of the parents. It is connected to ownership, caring, and parenting. Each name is associated with an event and identity. Those name givers are called indigenous people.

The indigenous people's voice against pro-rich development activities in India reflects their context and vision of life:

When the mountain disappears, what will be our identity?

If we leave our ancestral village, what will be our culture and spiritual identity?

If you do not allow us to cultivate, what will we eat? Do you want our children to die?

If you do not allow us to fish, how can we send our children to school?

If you do not allow us to practice shifting cultivation, what will be our religion and identity—our religion and identity are centered on the soil! How can we worship God?

If you do not allow us cultivate, what will we do the whole day?

When all the trees have been cut down, where will be the home of the animals and birds?

When all the waters are polluted, what will we drink? Do we have to buy water?

When all the air is unsafe to breathe, can we buy air?

The voices reflect the experience of pain and longing of indigenous people. They have suffered and continue to experience barbaric atrocities, human rights violations, ethnic conflict, poverty, injustice, low self-esteem, inferiority complexes, alienation from earth-centered life, and spirituality. In indigenous theology, this is a people whose history has been suppressed through different waves of invasion—Western colonization, Western religion and education, militarization, constitutional democracies, aid dependency, and economic globalization. Due to years of slavery and subjugation, indigenous people lost their self-esteem and gained a feeling of inferiority that prevails today.

In the globalized free market, the only people who count are those who have goods to sell and money to buy. This in turn drives many to the margins of economic life. The indigenous community who depends on land and forest resources has little chance to survive in this system. In short, globalization works for the benefit of the rich while the poor and indigenous become commodities, used as cheap labor. It has created a situation of marginalization, exclusion, and social disintegration. It is disheartening to see that the indigenous people are environmental prisoners in their own land.

Within nation states, the indigenous are also politically disenfranchised. Political oppression, militarization, and all forms of ethnocidal attack take place everyday. In search of a fuller life, justice, and equality, and to protect their identity and land, indigenous people have organized themselves to fight against the exploiters and oppressors. Violence, conflict, and killing become an everyday affair and reality. Everywhere we hear them reclaiming and reasserting their right to self-determination. All these are well-structured and institutionalized.

In this context, indigenous theology has to be collective solidarity resistance for defense of the oppressed. When oppression is structured and institutionalized, the collective solidarity resistance becomes the only weapon for the oppressed that can challenge the system. Collective solidarity resistance enters into the struggle of the defenseless people for radical change in the system of oppressive structures. It involves "struggling against systems and structures that disrupt the purpose of God for humanity and the whole of creation. Economic, political, social and religio-cultural barriers that are erected by powers have to be critiqued and rejected in the light of the principles of abundant life for all, regardless" (Rajkumar 2008, 167). Unless there is a change in the existing power relations in favor of the powerless, no justice will be achieved. Therefore, solidarity resistance is a matter of faith, a way of living girded with principles of love, equity, justice, and peace—for all (Rajkumar 2008, 172).

A Christian principle that affirms the collective solidarity resistance movement for celebration of life is found in the Trinitarian doctrine. Trinity is unity in community. They relate to each other, belong to one another, never insist on one's own way, and despite "their outward appearance of diversity," their foundational unity is still upheld. There is no dominion over another in the Trinity. Communion or togetherness is an integral feature in the very nature of God. Each divine person penetrates the other and allows himself/herself to be penetrated, each maintaining identity but sharing community (Abraham 2008, 11). Unity of equal partners bound by mutual love is a model that expresses divine reality. Our relationship with civil society and contextual theologies should express this model. We are united in diversity to resist the destructive forces and protect life.

The Bible is a book about the community's stories of their struggle against oppression and domination. The Exodus event is a collective experience of liberation. God's liberative activities—God's interventions, immediate, intimate encounter—take place in the community and not with an individual person. Individuals are called primarily to serve the community. "Let my people go" implies God is interested in community salvation. Liberation from Babylonian captivity is the goal of a group of people who have been oppressed and dehumanized. Jesus called a group of people to be his disciples and worked with them for the liberation of the poor, the women, the blind, the sick, and the sinners who have been excluded by society because of their social location.

For the prophets to know God is to do justice (Jer. 22:13–16). It is in justice done to the weak and helpless that Israel's true national identity is to be found. When power is misused to create, support, and promote injustice it is a denial of God. To believe in God is to turn from oneself and to commit one's life to God and to all men and women in concrete practice of justice. Silence in the face of an unjust system is denial of justice.

Indigenous theology attempts to mobilize community cutting across class, caste, tribe, and gender barriers to promote values and structure that enhance life, reject the forces and practices that destroy life, and liberate them from bondage. Collective solidarity resistance with the victims of the system and people in pain is witness to the liberating power of God in Christ. The cross is the sign of solidarity. To witness Christ without resistance for justice has no meaning.

Space Centered Liberation Theology

There are universal sets of values held by every society. Despite their cultural and ethnic diversity, indigenous communities all over the world share striking similarities. They uphold similar understandings of cosmology, religion, customs, ideology, and worldviews. More importantly, they all have a special relationship with their land[1]. Land, for them, is more than just a habitat or a political boundary; it is the basis of their social organization, economic system, and cultural identification. Naga wisdom goes like this:

The land is the Supreme Being's land
One cannot become rich by selling land

Do not be greedy for the land, if you want to live long
Land is life
The one who does not have land always cheats others or cannot become
    a good citizen
The land cries in the hands of greedy people
The land never lies; do not lie to the land
Anyone who takes another's land by giving false witness will not live long
The land is like a bird, it flies away soon in the hands of greedy people
You can sell other things, but not land
You are a stranger without land

A Maori poem begins:

Woman alone gives birth to mankind.
Land alone gives man his sustenance. (O'Grady 1981, 1)

Each expresses the spiritual relationship between the land and people.
The land is a complex spiritual component and occupies a central place
in the indigenous people's worldview. The land is not only sacred but
also cocreator with the Creator. (The Genesis account also speaks of
the earth as the cocreator of God. "Let the earth bring forth...." Gen.
1:24). It is the land that owns people and gives them an identity. It is
also a temple in and through which people become one not only with
the Sacred Power but also with their ancestors, the spirits, and other
living creatures. Political, economic, and social justice can be attained
only in relation to land.

Indigenous people's myths and rhetoric speak of the land as belonging to the Creator. Like the Hebrews ("the Earth is the Lord's and fullness thereof" [Ps. 24:1]), the indigenous people also affirm that the
land belongs to the Creator. The village, clans, and individuals own
the land only within the wider understanding that the land belongs to
the Creator. Thus, the land equally belongs to all with equal rights and
freedom to live in it. No one can claim it exclusively for himself/herself
nor can one sell it as though it is one's own exclusive property. In the
true sense, human ownership is only temporary. The whole land is the
home of the spirits and humans are only members in it.

Even the Supreme Being is understood in relation to land/space. For
example, the Aos and Sangtams of Nagaland (India) call their Supreme
Being, *Lijaba*. *Li* means "land" and *jaba* means "real." It means the
Supreme Being is "the real soil." Sometimes people call the Supreme
Being *Lizaba*. *Li* means "soil" and *zaba* means "enter," meaning "the one
who enters or indwells into the soil." People believe that the Supreme

Being enters into the soil with the seeds and rises again along with the crops. Thus, the blooming flower, bearing of fruits, and rice signifies the presence of the Creator. The whole creation is the manifestation of the Creator. This understanding reminds us of the Prophet Isaiah's vision. The Prophet heard God's messengers announcing that "the whole earth is full of God's glory" (Isa. 6:1–3). For indigenous people, there is no concept of the Creator without the land; the land and the Creator are inseparably related. The Creator indwells in human persons and in the soil.

Since land is the sustaining power, it is also an integral part of people's identity. It is not a mere space, but it is a place that gives an identity to the community. Without the land, there is no personhood and identity. If the land is lost, the family, clan, village, and the tribe's identity too will be lost. A person who is not deeply rooted in the land cannot become a good citizen. He/she is like a stranger without an identity and a home. It is usual for indigenous people to identify themselves with their village or tribe; a stranger rather than giving his/her name, gives the name of his/her village or tribe. The individual person's identity becomes subordinate to the community identity. The land is an integral part of people's identity.

The experience of time and history is also related to land. According to the indigenous concept, it is the land that creates time and history. People intimately move along with the soil cycle and surrounding environment. The festivals and religious activities are centered on the soil cycle. When the land and surrounding environment are destroyed, people experience a vacuum; the rhythm of life is seriously jeopardized. Rocks and boulders, trees and rivers are not just empty objects but religious objects; the voices and songs of animals speak of a religious language. The eclipse of the sun and of the moon is not simply a silent phenomenon of nature; it speaks to the community that observes it, often warning of impending danger and misfortune. It is in this milieu that people experience history and time. Thus, the concept of history and time is inseparably interlinked and rooted in the soil.

Unlike other great religions of the world, indigenous religion does not have any founder(s) or reformer(s) or guide(s) nor do people dance and sing adoring a divine historical person(s). They too have traditions of divine births and manifestations, but these are not worshipped. They have priests, officiating elders, diviners, and other famous men and women in the body of beliefs and mythologies that are respected and that form an integral part of their religious milieu, but they are neither worshipped nor adored as divine representatives. Instead, people dance and sing along with the cycle of land. A peculiar feature of indigenous religion is that the religious systems, ceremonies, rituals, festivals, and dances are centered and deeply rooted on the land itself.

Therefore, the concept of land is quite complex. "It is a heavily loaded term and combines together economics, politics, history, sociology, ethnicity, tradition, identity and spirituality" (Tuwere 2001, 39). In short, the land means survival. It is life. It is identity and spirituality. This understanding of the land is the common heritage of indigenous people all over the world. In the past, this understanding of land and other cultural values of indigenous people were considered "un-Christian." But, for indigenous people, the land has a profound theological meaning and a theology without taking into account this dimension will fail to address the hopes and longings of the people.

A crucial element missing from liberation theologies is the spiritual connection to the mystery of the earth's family. Rejection of this spiritual connection to earth's family in development activities is a serious mistake for the future survival of the world. Unless we rediscover our spiritual connection to the earth's family, it is not possible to talk about redemption of God's creation, liberation, and a community where all citizens are treated justly. This indigenous vision of life calls for a methodological shift in doing theology. It calls us to seek liberation from the perspective of "land" because it is the land that sustains and nourishes people and gives them an identity. Human liberation will be void and empty without affirming the integrity of the goodness of land and its resources. Liberation without land is not liberation. It will lead to slavery and destruction. This methodological priority of justice to land is essential not only because of indigenous peoples' "earth-centered" worldview and tradition but also because of our contemporary ecological crisis, misuse of resources, market culture, war for oil, and survival crisis of many people. This methodological priority of doing justice to the totality of creation challenges us to redefine the whole notion of Christian faith and praxis.

Indigenous People's Perspective on Liberation Theology

Indigenous people's theology is born out of the experiences of various forms of injustice and exploitation in the context of their assertion of rights and identity. It is a theology that attempts to express Christian faith in the sociocultural, religious, traditional, and liturgical thought patterns of the people. Indigenous peoples' theology is a liberation and resistance theology—to affirm justice, identity, dignity, and the wholeness of land and all its inhabitants. The experiences of oppressions and hardships, and their traditional stories, myths, symbols, dances, songs, and their connectedness to land and environment become vital resources for doing theology. It reflects on the issue of ethnic, cultural, and political identities of people from the subject of people, land, and sacred power to give them hope.

Initially, indigenous theology was greatly influenced and shaped by Latin American liberation methodology. Indigenous communities, women, and other marginalized movements have broadened the horizon of liberation theology from its Latin American impetus. Along with economic and political issues, the cultural and religious dimensions of discrimination are taken seriously in liberation theologies. They have influenced people to reread scripture from the perspective of the poor and oppressed in their struggle for justice and freedom. Commitment to the victims, the oppressed, and struggling poor as the basis and starting point of theology has inspired alienated indigenous people to discover their identity, rights, and dignity. It has motivated people to engage themselves in new ways of doing theology by relating the Gospel to the socio-politico-cultural realities.

Methodologically speaking, the point of departure of indigenous theology from other contextual theologies is that indigenous theology seeks liberation from the perspective of "space." In our search for liberation, the issue of space is central and crucial. As we affirmed earlier, a peculiar character of the indigenous worldview is that culture, religion, spirituality, and even the Supreme Being cannot be conceived without "creation/land" or "space." Humans always understand themselves as "an integral part of creation/land and not apart from it." Therefore, in the indigenous worldview, the issue of "space" is not merely one justice issue to be set alongside others. But it is the foundational theology of self-understanding out of which liberation, justice, and then peace will flow naturally and necessarily.[2] That means poverty, oppression, ethnic conflict, and identity issues cannot be understood without relating to the integrity of creation/land. Justice to creation/land is the key to liberation and human dignity and fullness of life. That is why harmony with the "land" is the starting point of indigenous people's theology and their search for liberation.

The first act of liberation is justice to creation itself. When we do justice to the land, then love, nurture, care, acceptance, and peace flow naturally and necessarily (Tinker 1994, 127–8). When there is justice in the land, the fields and forests and every living things will dance and sing for joy (Ps. 96: 11–12). Thus, an awareness of being one with the whole of creation is the spiritual foundation of indigenous people (Tinker 1994). Jurgen Moltmann (1979, 110–12) also argues that an authentic liberation can be experienced only when we take into consideration the following levels: (1) struggles for economic justice against the exploitation of humans, (2) struggles for human dignity and human rights against political oppression of humans, (3) struggle for peace with nature against the industrial destruction of the environment, and (4) struggles for hope against apathy in asserting the significance of the whole in personal life. Indigenous people throughout their histories have affirmed this interrelationship of poverty, political oppression, economic exploitation, and justice to land. In different forums, indigenous people have made it clear that the question of identity, hunger, diseases, illiteracy, culture, and religion are inseparably related to space and the survival of indigenous people is an integral part of total cosmic justice.

Therefore, from indigenous people's perspective, one cannot do theology without relating to the issue of "space." A theology that addresses humanity alone and emphasizes soul-winning but leaves the rest of the cosmos unaddressed is an incomplete theology. Theology becomes impotent when it addresses only humanity. There is no theological and biblical justification to reduce theology to mere liberative or transformative activity of humanity. Therefore, the challenge before us is to commit ourselves to struggle for the transformation of the poor, the weak, and disfigured humanity and to curtail the overexploitation of nature. Without restoring justice to space, the indigenous and oppressed communities will not be able to attain liberation and fullness of life in Christ.

The core of human suffering is inseparably connected to the violation of space: our selfishness, greed, and exploitative attitude toward our mother earth brings poverty, oppression, ethnic conflict, and many other forms of injustice. The moment we cut ourselves off from reverential relationships with the land, we are uprooted from the world of mystery and we live a life of indecency. Never-ending exploitation of a limited earth's resources means a few economic affluent individuals cause the majority of the poor to live with misery and hunger. This disparity makes everyone turn against each other; everyone becomes a threat to the other's peaceful existence. This happens state-wise, nationally, and locally. Suspicion, doubt, and selfishness take precedence over trust, love, care, and acceptance. Our rootlessness makes life lose meaning and purpose (Kochappilly 1999).

We need to reexamine our wrong orientation toward the mystery of nature. With advancements in science, people believe that there is nothing amazing about the cosmos. The physical world is viewed merely as a sum-total of many material components and energies. Humans can understand, predict, and control everything. We are separated from, and master of, earth. Nature is something "out there," apart from us and also apart from God. This wrong notion justifies manipulation and domination of land and its resources. Without any religious restraints, the land and its resources are exploited and abused, denying the right of everybody. Today the land and natural resources that sustained life for centuries are forcibly taken away in the name of development without proper alternatives. Indigenous people have not only lost their soil-centered culture but have also been reduced to bonded laborers on their own land.

And finally, we lack a proper orientation to God who is the source and the sovereign Lord of all creation. Instead of affirming the Divine presence in the universe, human beings consider themselves as the lord and master of all. Every person wants to control and manipulate the land and its resources threatening the rhythm of the universe. "Therefore, the land mourns and all who dwell in it languish and also beasts of field and the birds of the air and even the fish of the sea are taken away" (Hosea 4: 3). The attempt by the servant to take over the place of the Master at home provokes other servants who are also struggling for lordship and the home becomes a battlefield. No one is at peace. Therefore, for indigenous people, doing justice to land is the foundation for life. When we do justice to God's world, people will find a healthier life.

Notes

1. When we say "space," "creation," or "land" it means a place, a sacred place, which gives us an identity and sustenance. It includes all beings.
2. For this insight, I owe deep gratitude to Tink Tinker's (1981, 1994) articles.

Bibliography

Abraham, K. C. 2008. "Living in a Religiously Plural World—Problems and Challenges for Doing Mission in Asia." *JTCA* 7&8, 3–14.

Kochappilly, P. P. 1999. *Celebrative Ethics: Ecological Issues in the Light of the Syro-Malabar Qurbana.* Bangalore: Dharmaram.

Moltmann, J. 1979. *The Future of Creation.* London: SCM.

O'Grady, A., ed. 1981. *Inheritors of the Earth.* Hong Kong: URM, Christian Conference of Asia.

Rajkumar, E. 2008. "Theology of Resistance." In *Light on Our Dusty Path: Essays for Bible Lovers,* ed. Israel Selvanagayam, 160–75. Bangalore: BTESSC/SATHRI.

Tinker, G. 1981. "American Indian & the Art of the Land." In *Voices from the Third World* 14:2 (December), 22–38

———. 1994. "Spirituality and Native American Personhood: Sovereignty & Solidarity." In *Spirituality of the Third World,* ed. K. C. Abraham and Barnedatte Mbuy, 125–36. Maryknoll: Orbis Books.

Tuwere, S. 2001. "Indigenous People's Struggle for Land and Identity." In *Pacific Journal of Theology, Series II, Issue 25,* 39–50.

CHAPTER 13

Embodied Theology: Indigenous Wisdom as Liberation

Sylvia Marcos
smarcost@gmail.com

How can we define *Teologia India* (indigenous theology)? What makes it different to *Teologia de la Liberación* (liberation theology)? Even though both "theologies" are centered on a preferential option for the poor and the indigenous peoples as subjects of faith, *Teologia India*, or *Sabiduria India* (indigenous wisdom), as many of the local pastoral actors prefer to call it, goes beyond liberation theology, complementing Catholic liturgy with practices and reflections on faith based on Mesoamerican philosophical heritages.

This innovative theological project is grounded in a serious and respectful relationship with indigenous Mayan communities. These peoples or *pueblos* belong to the Catholic diocese and are included in its pastoral work in San Cristobal de las Casas, Chiapas, Mexico. Much of what I will review here springs from a long interview I did with Don Samuel Ruiz, the late bishop emeritus of the regional diocese, who worked in San Cristobal for more than 40 years[1] (Marcos 1998b). I will also bring forth some of my own systematizations on "embodied thought" (Marcos 1998a) and some lessons learned from my extended presence in the region. Since 1974, when I was first invited by Ruiz to come to the diocese, I have been loosely but regularly connected to the grassroots projects of *Teologia India* and autochthonous churches in Chiapas.

This Catholic proposal is evolving quietly, offering new insights on faith and how we can live together and sustain the earth as well as respect the plurality of the diverse religious and cultural practices and beliefs present in the area. A fresh Catholic Church, innovative and committed to social justice is emerging. Chiapas is a tiny point on earth, but it is pregnant with hope.

Theology as a Constellation of Practices: A Ceremony in the Forest of Chiapas

O You by whom we live and move, nothing we say here is real. What we say on this earth is like a dream. We only mutter like one waking from sleep. (Bierhorst 1985, 170)

Ipalnemohuani is the God through whom we live. (Netzahualcoyotl quoted in Leon- Portilla 1990, 7)[2]

"Tloquenahuaque" is the Lord of close vicinity, del "cerca y del junto." (Leon-Portilla 1990, 63)

I arrive invited to the mass in celebration of the eighteenth anniversary of *Universidad de la Tierra* (CIDECI) in San Cristobal de las Casas. The *ermita* (chapel) is full. I can see a crowd gathering at the altar. At the side of the bishop stand the priests that will co-celebrate and beside them, a man and his wife, elderly Tzotzil Mayan people. They are *tunnhel* (deacons). Man and woman as a unit incarnate the Mesoamerican concept of "duality" and will contribute as co-ministers in the ceremonial mass. Dressed in their local attire, they stand proudly by the side of the bishop.

The music we hear in this Catholic mass is the ritualistic sacred music of the surrounding indigenous hamlets. We can recognize the structure of the Eucharist, although we could easily be distracted by the splashes of color, the languid repetitious rhythm of indigenous sacred tunes, and the collectivity that ministers the mass. Several priests and ordained indigenous deacons populate the higher space of the chapel. The readers of the scriptures are women and they read in three languages: Spanish, Tzotzil, and Tzeltal. Who leads the ritual? I would answer: the collectivity.

In this very concrete experience, many of the tenets of *Teologia India*, and of the project of "autochthonous churches," are perceptible even to an unprepared onlooker as "excerpts of practice." The pastoral work of the diocese of Chiapas grows and develops ever more toward a respect and recognition of the values, spirituality, devotions, and ritual practices of the region's indigenous peoples. In what follows, I hope to present not a finished analysis of a stable reality but a study reflecting the fuzziness of reality and the process of permanent change.

Colonial Influences

We should be attuned to the ways in which native peoples adapted to their colonial circumstances, accommodated the Christian hierarchy, and absorbed and synthesized new ideas and beliefs. On the basis of being a distinct people (Warren and Jackson 2002, 13), they assert a common past, which has been in part suppressed, in part fragmented, by colonialism. They participate in the emergence of a cultural revitalization that reunites the past with the present as a political and religious force. We are witnessing the transformation of indigenous religion itself, not forcedly through conversion and hybridization, and even less through "merchandization" (commodification), but through its own internal process of metamorphoses and migrations.

The term religion was, according to Jonathan Smith, first "extended to non-Christian examples in the literature of exploration particularly in descriptions of the complex civilizations of Mesoamerica" (Smith 1998, 270). However, in contrast to the Christianity imported by the Spaniards, indigenous Mayan conceptual systems are formed by a complex web of epistemic particularities. Among others we find: concepts of time/place, gender, nature, self/community embedded in particular cultural perceptions.

The Epistemic Context of *Teologia India*

Knowledge systems pervade our thinking, influence our conceptions of causality, and guide our sensory perceptions. At all times, we are immersed in an epistemic system that organizes the way we conceptualize the material world around us to "fit" this cognitive system (Marcos 1988). When we approach *Teologia India or Sabiduria India*, we can discern the underlying cognitive structure, which is intimately bound to indigenous cosmology. Some particularities of these indigenous traditions are concepts of nature and of the divine in which a merging of transcendence and immanence occurs, a belief in a bidirectional flow of spiritual forces between the realm of the deities and human existence, metaphors as the selected vehicles for conveying hermetic meanings, and beliefs that are *embodied* and thus articulated implicitly rather than explicitly. "The word comes and goes, goes and returns, the word walks . . . to achieve unity say the indigenous"[3] (Alicia Gomez quoted in Ruiz with Torner 2003, 79).

Both Pierre Bourdieu and Michel Foucault have written about the quiet way in which an epistemic configuration can operate and express itself. It "quietly" takes on existence through practices, through actions. The *epistemè* is embodied and thus exists. "Actions can supply moments of reinterpretation and reformulation" (Bourdieu cited in Moore 1994, 155). Belief and thought enact themselves through corporeality. Without physicality, there is no sustenance and foundational reality for ideas, beliefs, thoughts, and especially for "reflections on faith." Here we can grasp the main tenets of indigenous spirituality and thus of the intercultural project of *Teologia India*. We could call it an *Embodied Theology*.

Its embodied character is also the reason why it is often perceived from the outside as a variable set *of practices*. Ruiz affirms that "the indigenous people prefer the term '*sabiduría*' (wisdom) to theology: '*sabiduría india*.'" He adds, "Theology is systematic, abstract . . . ," (and I could add *disembodied*) " . . . this abstraction is foreign to the Indians [. . .], who live a communal life. They nourish themselves from contemplation and reflections on nature, myths, and dreams" (Marcos 1998b, 48–52).

Dreaming as Prophecy

Thinking about the meaning of/and place of dreams in indigenous Tzotzil communities, Ruiz adds:

> The Acteal local inhabitants who had been displaced from their hamlet,[4] they had decided to return home. But some of them had dreams, premonitions. Actually it was an old woman and old man and three others. The five of them agreed in interpreting those dreams as an omen. "This is not the opportune time to return, . . . We can not go back now." (Marcos 1998b, 33)

For the local people, dreams are encoded messages. Dreams are communications from wise ancestral protecting spirits. Don Samuel heard the indigenous interpretations; he understood and valued them in their indigenous context. He even called the dreams "prophetic" and advised to follow them (Marcos 1998b, 3). The people did not return to their hamlet at that time.[5]

Myths Weaving History

Myths are history, a history that gets constructed and reconstructed permanently. Myths are considered facts. Don Samuel tells me about the story of a grain of coffee being given to the peoples there by "el Señor" in the origins of time, to help them in their survival. But it is well known that coffee was brought to the region in the early years of last century. How to interpret this?

> Through a telling or a re-telling of their myths, indigenous people enact a reflection or and "indigenous wisdom" that has been transmitted through their elders...the sources from which this presence of God is perceptible spring form within the confines of indigenous culture...the reflection which derives from that is not as among us based in philosophy, but rather in mythology. Myth is a form of "abstract" reflection about things." (Marcos 2001, 33)

Paraphrasing Diane Bell, "The body of wisdom often called 'myths' by outsiders, for the Mayans is a matter of fact" (1997, 53).

A Debt the Church Should Honor

Ruiz smiles and looks at me challengingly. "The Gospel did not arrive to America with Christopher Colombus' three caravels. God was here before."

> One can never overemphasize the importance of indigenous reflection. It initiates a dialogue that never took place in the five hundred years since the first evangelization. A foreign culture was imposed over the indigenous culture in order to express the gospel. There was no reciprocal listening...it was not possible to recognize anything positive in a religion that was not Christian....simply, that which was indigenous had no value and had to be eradicated. Only now, after Vatican II we are commencing to correct this serious error. (Marcos 2001, 3)

Ruiz (2003) often speaks about "how the indigenous converted me.". The evident irony of the power inversion implied in this expression gives a clue into the depth of his commitment to amend the Catholic Church's presence and evangelization in Mexico.

Embodied Theology

I have analyzed one of the main characteristics of Mesoamerican Mayan thought, a thought that is not built on mutually exclusive categories. A thought that does not separate matter from spirit, earth from sky, death from life; a thought that is embodied or incarnate (Marcos 1998a). One of its main characteristics is the perception of things in flux, both flowing and "fusing." This notion of a continuous flux between the material and the spiritual, of a permanent oscillation between the two poles of a duality is basic to a deep understanding of the proposals of *Teologia India* that can best be perceived as a "constellation of practices."

These practices include not only the rhythms of local indigenous music, the chanting, dancing, and rituals like *el caracol*[6] but also the veneration of deities inside caves and the rituals on the sacred space on mountain tops. These practices of *Teologia India*, cannot be fully comprehended by a pastoral work inspired by the conventional Christian strategies of "inculturation," defined as the missionary project of incorporating indigenous music and art into Catholic liturgy (Gifford 2007, 122). A deeper effort is now taking place. It includes joint reflection on faith, consultation of elders (women and men) considered the bearers of the indigenous religious traditions.

> *Teologia india* is a way of reuniting the strength of God, the strength of the elders, and thanks to this strength, confronting conflicts and Keeling hope. It is the indigenous themselves who do this work. It is they who speak with the elders.... Each community has a Group of theologians, who speak with the elders who tell them the ancient words.[7] (Gomez quoted in Ruiz with Torner 2003, 79)

This commitment is far beyond the "preferential option for the poor," one of the basic tenets of liberation theology. Indigenous theology commits itself to respecting the epistemic and philosophical backgrounds of the Mayan cosmos and to building a "theological" perspective in harmony with it. The Christian philosophical religious tradition that came with the missionaries was plagued by a disdain for matter and rejection of earthly dimensions contradictory to the pristine Christian faith in the Incarnation. Catholics committed to Indian wisdom move away from these disincarnate conceptions, to accommodate a universe where earth and matter are sacred, where natural beings express divinity and where the spiritual and the material are not separated.

According to the Mayan vision of the cosmos, human life is intimately connected with its surroundings. All surroundings have life, so they become sacred. We encounter earth, mountains, valleys, caves, plants, animals, stones, water, air, moon, sun, stars, which share in sacredness (Hunt 1977). In the words of Carlos Camarena, a Jesuit at the Bachajon Mission in Chiapas since 1963: "For the indigenous peoples material and spiritual realities are the same"[8] (quoted in Ruiz with Torner 2003,

88). Eugenio Maurer, a Jesuit parish priest committed to the indigenous populations says:

> For the people of Guaquitepec all mountains are "alive" in that they are the font of life: they are the site of cornfields; firewood comes from their slopes; springs emerge from them...they are the dwelling place of important sacred beings...they have power in their own right. (Quoted in Gossen and Leon-Portilla 1997, 232)

For indigenous peoples, the world is not "out there," established outside of and apart from them. It is within them and even "through" them. *Teologia India* tells this explicitly. It is not an abstract reflection springing from pure spirit or pure mind. It is grounded; it is practices, actions, rituals, devotions, processions, embroidering, dancing, and chanting. All these actions have to be incarnated into bodies that are themselves a vortex of emanations and inclusions from the material as well as the nonmaterial world. As such, carnal bodies are intertwined in the divine and belong to the sacred domain (Marcos 1998a).

"Here you cannot distinguish between God and the world, between God and his creation"[9] (Andres Aubry quoted in Ruiz with Torner 2003, 63). Thus, *Teologia India* has to be found in the myriad incarnated and corporeal ways by which the indigenous peoples express their beliefs. "The indigenous cultures are characterized by their unity," says Andrés Aubry, and he adds: "Unity also between death and life"[10] (quoted in Ruiz with Torner 2003, 67). Here again, we find the duality and fluid oscillation between opposed and complementary poles (Marcos 2006).

Indigenous Languages

The conceptual source of *Teologia India*, springs from local indigenous languages. Aubry affirms that "a language is a conceptual system"[11] (quoted in Ruiz with Torner 2003, 63). He gives, as an example that in Tzotzil, there is no word for the verb "*ser*." To take a Spanish "equivalent," let's consider the verb *estar* in its differences with *ser*. "*Estar*" means "being in relation" to someone else or to a situation or to the natural surroundings (*entorno*). There is no concept of an ontology where a being is conceived by itself, alone, individual, separate.

Teologia India is greatly enhanced by the use of terms, meanings, and syntactic turns proper to indigenous Mayan languages. *Teologia India* in Chiapas could not be grasped without those languages that provide it with its foundation. The pastoral work of the diocese makes permanent use of one or several of those languages allowing for their particular conceptual meanings to inform its commitments and work.

Indian Theology as an Outcome

"*Teologia India* is the final result of a pastoral action"[12] (Marcos 2001). *Teologia India* and its practices do not stem from a project started by the will of the bishop, the priests, nuns, and the pastoral agents at the diocese of San Cristobal. They did not sit together to discuss and decide how it had to be done. It is the result of their pastoral approach with indigenous communities and of their respect and awe for the indigenous religious universes. These indigenous universes are so elusive, so rich, and have been discarded in the past. It is the end result of many years of getting close to the indigenous peoples and communities with an attuned ear, a respectful attention, and a congenial attitude. Especially vital is the attitude of pastoral actors, listening and learning to absorb indigenous epistemic worlds and how to work with and through them. Perhaps hidden is the idea, that I venture here as my own, that the pastoral agents—nuns and priests and the bishop himself—could discover a way of feeling and conceiving God that would also enrich their own.

The Collective Way of Understanding God

Teologia India is and must be a collective experience. It is practiced within the collective corporeality and embeddedness of liturgies.[13] Historically, Christianity has a strong communitarian sense, and early Christian assemblies have been a model and are always at the background of our hopes for a better Catholic community. Yet, the indigenous lived experiences of community are grounded on a concept of collectivity hard to understand for the Westernized mentality. It is easy to be entranced by the ways we see them acting, living, and believing through community. It stands out as an ideal. Some of the first Catholic missionaries that arrived in the Americas agreed describing these communitarian ties as "the Christianity of the Indians."[14]

To indigenous peoples, even today, a community is not conceived as a collectivity of individuals, according to the Western scheme exposed by Louis Dumont in his *Essays on Individualism* (1992). For the Westernized mentality, a whole (Greek *holon*) is a collection of individuals (Greek *atomoi*); accordingly, Europeans, North Americans, and Westernized Mexicans are trapped in an *atomistic holism* that renders notions of the person as node of a network of relations and of one's place in the world as a *topos in a cosmos* (or *tlalticpac*) ungraspable. For the indigenous Mesoamericans, the full person has always in him/herself parts of the collectivity: the *calpulli*, the *Junta de Buen Gobierno*, the *pueblo*. It means that a part of him/herself belongs to the collectivity of which s/he is a part. The person is not complete without that part. If it were missing, he or she would experience it as the loss of a "limb" or another vital entity without which he or she lacks integrality and coherence as a human being.

The embeddedness of the person in the collective cannot be equated to the consideration of the *ego* as a totally separate individual being, body, and soul. With our concepts of the unitary soul or unitary identity or unitary subjectivity, we are unable to approach in depth what collectivity means for the indigenous people. We can only try.

In Catholic faith–based organizations such as "Las Abejas" (the Bees), we can detect the kind of communitarianism that pervades the indigenous worlds. Their cellular structure, as in the case of Acteal (municipality of Chenhalo),[15] allows for maximum flexibility. They are one of the most visible outcomes of the outreach of pastoral work of the diocese. This cellular collective structure enables the constituent organizations to shift arenas modifying their strategies in response to attacks by the federal and state police and paramilitary forces. It permitted the collective mode of organization to extend to regions. Indigenous peoples in the self-constituted autonomous regions of Northern Chiapas and the Lacandon rainforest as well as bordering hamlets of highland municipalities (*municipios autónomos*) are in fact engaged in the practice of collective autonomy while waiting for the government to implement the San Andrés Accords (Nash 2001).

The diocesan pastoral work sustains and builds around these indigenous practices. Spirituality is linked to a communitarian sense in which all beings are interrelated and complement each other. These are some of the spiritual and political practices that have been linked to the Pan-Mayan movement (Nash 2001).

As June Nash affirms, the indigenous people are seeking autonomy in daily practice through the "*Juntas de buen gobierno*," operating within an indigenous collectivity governing themselves in traditional territories. Through the practices of "*mandar obedeciendo*" (obeying we lead), one could easily think of the early Christian communities being embodied in contemporary practices by these indigenous rebels and their supporters.

Final Reflections

Beyond inculturation, the diocesan pastoral work in Chiapas threads a new path to build a true intercultural dialogue that we may call *Teologia India* or *Sabiduria India*. It is based on a constellation of practices, which have to be understood in the context of the interconnection between matter and spirit, of the embodied sacredness of beings, of earth, nature, and humans and on the epistemic philosophical backbone of the indigenous communities. This is the Catholic Church in Chiapas: balancing faith and politics, theology and justice, devotion and rights, mind and bodies, orthodoxy and inculturation.

Notes

1. Ruiz was a key political defender of the Mayan indigenous populations in his dioceses in the southeast state of Chiapas, Mexico. He and his collaborators developed a *pastoral indigena* that allowed him to propose and coin the term Teologia India during his more than 40 years of tenure at the dioceses of San Cristobal de las Casas, Chiapas.
2. Netzahualcoyotl was a thirteenth century Toltec chief and poet.
3. "*La palabra va y viene, se va y vuelve, la palabra camina...para alcanzar la unidad dicen los indígenas.*"
4. He is referring to the massacre of 45 people, members of the community of *Las Abejas,* perpetrated by paramilitaries backed by the State government.
5. Although it is beside the point I am making here, it was the best decision possible at that time in that situation (Marcos 1998b).
6. In ancient Mesoamerica deep sea shells were the symbol of a new beginning.
7. "*La teologia India es una manera de reunir la fuerza de Dios, la fuerza de los abuelos, y gracias a esta fuerza, hacer frente a los conflictos y conservar la esperanza. Son los propios indígenas los que hacen el trabajo. Son ellos los que hablan con los abuelos... Cada comunidad tiene un grupo de teologos, hablan con los abuelos que les cuentan las antiguas palabras.*"
8. "*Para los indígenas, las realidades espirituales y materiales son lo mismo*"
9. "*Aqui no se puede distinguir entre Dios y el mundo, entre Dios y su obra.*"
10. "*La culturas indígenas se caracterizan por su unidad... unidad también entre la muerte y la vida.*"
11. "*...affirmo que una lengua es un sistema conceptual.*"
12. *Teologia India es el resultado final de una acción pastoral.*
13. This is why Ruiz was adamant about not allowing anyone to interview him alone about Teologia India. He insisted in his book *Como me convirtieron los indígenas* that several pastoral agents be interviewed alongside him.
14. Some of these early colonial sources are Fray Bernadino de Sahabun, Fray Diego Duran, and Motolinia, who admired the collective cohesion and sharing of the local indigenous peoples they were catechizing.

15. As noted above, 45 members of the community of *Las Abejas* were massacred.

Bibliography

Bell, D. 1997. "Desperately Seeking Redemption." *Worlds of the Shaman, Natural History* 106:2, 53.

Bierhorst, J. 1985. *Cantares Mexicanos Songs of the Aztecs.* Stanford: Stanford University Press.

Dumont, L. 1992. *Essays on Individualism : Modern Ideology in Anthropological Perspective.* Chicago : University of Chicago Press.

Gifford, P. 2007. "The Nature and Effects of Mission Today: A Case Study from Kenya." *Social Sciences and Missions* 20, 117–47. Einvandewereld: Brill.

Gossen, G., and M. Leon-Portilla. 1997. *South and Meso-American Spirituality: From the Cult of the Feathered Serpent to the Theology of Liberation.* New York: Crossroad.

Hunt, E. 1977. *The Transformation of the Hummingbird: Cultural Roots of a Zinacantecan Mythical poem.* New York: Cornell University Press.

Leon-Portilla, M. 1969. *Pre-Columbian Literatures of Mexico.* Norman: University of Oklahoma Press.

———. 1990. *Aztec Thought and Culture.* Norman: University of Oklahoma Press.

Marcos, S. 1988. "Cognitive Structures and Medicine." *Curare* 11, 87–96. Wiesbaden: Vieweg & Sohn Verlag.

———. 1998a. "Embodied Religious Thought: Gender Categories in Mesoamerica." *Religion* 28, 371–82.

———. 1998b. "Las Semillas del Verbo en la Sabiduria India," interview of Don Samuel Ruiz. *Revista Académica para el Estudio de las Religiones*, Tomo II: *Chiapas el Factor Religioso*, 33–59.

———. 2001. *The Seeds of the Word in Indigenous Wisdom,* interview with D. Samuel Ruiz, trans. Jean Robert. Unpublished.

———. 2006. *Taken from the Lips: Gender and Eros in Mesoamerican Religions.* Boston: Brill Academic Press.

Moore, H. 1994. *A Passion for Difference: Essays in Anthropology and Gender.* Bloomington: Indiana University Press.

Nash, J. 2001. *Mayan Visions: The Quest for Autonomy in an Age of Globalization.* New York: Routledge.

Ruiz, S. 2003. *Como me convirtieron los indigenas,* with Carlos Torner. Santander: Sal Terrae; Cantabria.

Smith, J. 1998. "Religion, Religions, Religious." In *Critical Terms for Religious Studies*, ed. Mark Taylor, 269–84. Chicago: University of Chicago Press.

Warren, K., and J. E. Jackson. 2002. *Indigenous Movements, Self-Representation and the State in Latin America.* Austin: University of Texas Press.

PART IV

Practice

CHAPTER 14

What Does Liberation Theology Mean in and for the Twenty-First Century?

Jenny Plane Te Paa
jenzat1@gmail.com

B eginning in the mid-1980s, as a thirty-something year old, I was a relative latecomer to the academic study of theology. Being lay, I was consistently reminded by my ordained peers, of my "curiosity" value within the academy!

In my previous professional incarnations I had worked as a social worker, a student counselor, and as a teacher. I also had broad experience in community development and in high-level social policy development at local and national government levels.

In my previous sociopolitical incarnations, I had since the early 1970s been deeply embroiled in the emergent Maori activist movement for political change. This was a movement, which ultimately sought and then in no small measure, ultimately succeeded with shaming the nation Aotearoa New Zealand into recognizing, into confronting, and then, very tentatively, into beginning to redeem its appalling legacy of "imperialist racism!"

In my continuous religious incarnation, I was and am still a baptized lifelong actively committed lay Anglican.

In the mid-1980s all of my third decade planets and astrological signs aligned themselves, doubtless with the celestial intervention of some among the great cloud of witnesses. It was during this period I found myself very unexpectedly called to a leadership role within my church. This was a role that required someone with "professional skills in teaching, educational administration and pastoral care, someone with a strong social justice analysis, someone who understood the Gospel imperatives for bold discipleship and prophetic witness, someone with a credible academic background in theology!"

According to the Maori male church leaders, tribal elders, and all, who "anointed" and appointed me to the leadership role, I had all the prerequisite skills and qualifications. According to me, I lacked deep and very necessary theological literacy, and so I went back to school to learn deeply and broadly of the things of God.

Through my postgraduate research work I quickly realized that my elders' insistence about my "sufficiency" in terms of theological prepared-ness was in the most potent and ultimately poignant of ways a projection of the mask of "academic" pretense they had all learned to wear so well.

Pretense, that in the late twentieth and early twenty-first century, strong cultural identity coupled with the badge of their ordination was of far greater significance than any "white western" endorsement of their intellectual prowess. Culturally based anti-intellectualism had thus become such an intimidating rebuttal in postcolonial race politics.

Sadly too I soon discovered in my historical survey that from the earliest times of Maori Anglicans seeking to be formally theologically educated (around 1843), without exception, the outcome for virtually all was unquestionably one of significant academic "insufficiency."

You may have noticed I have not added in an end date here—this is because to the largest extent the situation remains unchanged. I will return to this point presently.

Twenty years ago, deficit model education was omnipresent in the theological academy as I was to discover for myself at first hand as I endeavored to begin to "study theology."

As a lay indigenous woman I had impressive professional qualifica-tions and vast activist experience particularly in working among the poor, the hungry, the outcasts, and the prisoners. As an ecclesiologically articulate Anglican woman with a strong record of church service, it was such an extraordinarily bewildering experience to find myself in the mid-1980s, being regarded and subsequently being related to as a rela-tive freak, in the hallowed halls of the theological academy!

Even being a faith-filled Anglican in a postcolonial nation still inex-tricably wedded to the vestiges and trappings of its inglorious imperial past did not afford me any advantageous inside running in the nation-ally dominant and (even by global standards) extraordinarily well endowed Anglican seminary!

Fortunately, mine was an ecumenical degree, and given my profes-sional background, I chose to take all the social teachings papers, which were of course only on offer from the Catholic seminary.

Thanks be to God I very quickly found Gustavo Gutiérrez and Jon Sobrino, Jose Miguez Bonino and Juan Luis Segundo, Bartolome de las Casas and Leonardo and Clodovis Boff.[1] I loved them all deeply and appreciatively because they spoke (at least initially) into my indigenous situation with ease and with accuracy. I searched and searched in vain for the women who had doubtless been their informants and advisors, their helpmates and nurturers; sadly I was not to find them mentioned or acknowledged anywhere.

At first though, all that mattered to me as an already well-educated indigenous person was that liberation theology provided me with the discourse and the rhetoric of transformative justice, the insistence upon economic and sociopolitical analysis, the Gospel frameworks for doing God's justice, and the glorious prospect of freedom for those oppressed. As an activist myself I felt vindicated.

I kept returning however to thinking about those of my forefathers—to thinking about all those generations of indigenous Maori priests and deacons, those for whom the experience of being in seminary-based theological education had been so systemically culturally demeaning. Would liberation theology have helped? Would they, like me, have felt vindicated?

I kept thinking about the intellectual indignity of their clerical status—ordained but not necessarily "qualified." I wondered how they themselves really felt? I wondered why I had never really thought critically about the obvious institutionally imposed limitations of their utterly self-sacrificial pastoral ministries among Maori people, among those politically and thus economically doomed as with all colonized indigenous peoples, to marginal lives of poverty and powerlessness.

Yes my forefather priests and deacons were irrefutably the finest exemplars of Christian witness. They showed infinite mercy. They showed kindness. They were excruciatingly humble. And they were dearly loved and highly respected in our tribal communities. And yet their superbly selfless essentially pastoral interventions could only ever be palliative at best, inadvertently patronizing at worst.

For they were unable to speak effectively and prophetically about, or to act effectively and strategically against, the inexorable socioeconomic march of neo-capitalism, of neoliberalism; let alone to know how best to effectively resist various other contemporary modes of social production, to name and shame all of those things that invariably impact with disproportionate negativity upon the lives of those already so disadvantaged.

And all of this "limitation" I saw as educational not intellectual. This limitation I figured was because the always foreboding and inhospitable seminary environment within which teaching occurred was combined with the monolingual and monocultural theology they were taught with. The often culturally insensitive way they were taught had culturally humiliated my forefathers by systematically discrediting and disallowing Maori epistemology, Maori ways of knowing, of thinking, of experiencing, or of understanding the things of God.

The *wairua* or spiritual strength of Maori students was very quickly diminished. This educational limitation had domesticated them ecclesially. It had rendered them passive to the authority of those whose benevolent racism assuredly reminded Maori clergy of their permanently underclass ecclesial status. It taught Maori not to challenge episcopal authority and thus not to challenge secular authority either. Finally this educational limitation had disenfranchised them intellectually by not developing their capacity for critical thought, by not integrating and politicizing the things of the public square into the theological curriculum, by not modeling teaching as being the sacred art of molding and shaping and celebrating the incalculably precious life of the mind.

And so it was that around 15 years ago, that I first glimpsed what I only now recognize was a Holy Spirit moment writ large for me!

I was at that time as a junior lecturer and as a PhD student puzzling mightily about what on earth as a formerly upwardly mobile secular professional I was actually doing in theological education! Secondly I was nonetheless a committed Christian indigenous layperson working away at a critical analysis of the historically embedded situation of Maori theological educational failure. Implicated in the evidential statistics of this so-called educational failure at St. Johns College, was my own grandfather who was a student of the College from 1927 until 1928. Chosen by the tribe to become a priest, he was an extraordinarily gifted young man and a widely acknowledged future leader. In spite of his being "failed" in the hands of the college he went on to become one of New Zealand's most well-known indigenous elders. My grandfather Ephraim was a tribal leader renowned throughout the land as erudite scholarly gentleman, as peacemaker, and as highly respected religious leader.

And so it was for me in that Holy Spirit moment of puzzlement and outrage that I began to reflect on the rhetoric, the grand redemptive justice claims of the liberation theology I had studied and from which I had gained such encouragement. I wondered in that moment, seriously wondered, that if the problem for my forefathers was educational, then what role might liberation theology as an ideological construct, as a theological tool, as an educational framework, might have to play in my naïve determination to single-handedly transform theological education! My project then was first to rid it of its inherent institutional racism and, in so doing, to redeem it from its historically established and deeply embedded structural, attitudinal, and perversely anti-intellectual injustices!

And so it was that I began to take myself seriously and to do some critical thinking around if, how, why, when, for whom, liberation theology might assist as redemptive, transformative educational tool for indigenous and Third World students in my context. I soon began of necessity to also rethink my initial and totally uncritical enchantment with liberation theology. Even as it had surely been the balm of Gilead for me in the early days of my own struggles to be accepted within the theology academy.

Let me explain. I had as previously mentioned, always noticed that liberation theology maintained an unapologetic silence on many issues of gender justice. I had already noticed and experienced at first hand one very negative outcome of liberation theology's well-meaning contribution, which enabled an extraordinary upsurge in cultural pride as previously colonized indigenous peoples began our pushback against the destructive and utterly disempowering legacies of imperialism. In this latter instance, indigenous male dominance and blatant chauvinism, often masquerading as recovered cultural tradition, flourished. Liberation theology had no comment to make about the resultant gender injustice experienced by indigenous women! Then there was also the matter of classism and of who has benefited most from the incorporation of liberation theology into the Western academy?

Liberation theology then, I figure now needs liberating from its own institutionalized limitations. It lacks attention to issues of justice for women. It is slow in responding to increasing global critiques of its economic assumptions. It avoids the chauvinism inherent in all tribalisms. Its own professional academic reality is class-ridden. These are just some of the limitations being noticed.

Who are the authentically liberative liberation theologians of our times? Where are the institutions that are intentionally targeting, gathering, and mentoring the next generations of underside scholars and leaders in the same ways that feminists have modeled for years? Where are the examples of radical institutional transformation that would inevitably occur as a new generation of indigenous and third world liberation theologians and their communities are authentically embraced by the theological academy?

Of course there are examples, but are these proportionate to the degree of suffering experienced by those for whom the sociopolitical and spiritual impact of liberation theology is intended?

Ivan Petrella,[2] is one of the few contemporary liberation theology scholars I discern is taking time to consider some of these issues. Especially Petrella notices, and I think names correctly in the first of his two theses on expanding the scope of liberation theology, that for example the uncritical privileging and single identity ghettoizing of particularity must be discouraged, if not subsumed in preference to the transcendent universal.

I agree even as I recognize that there are of course very real risks inherent in this proposition not least to those precious and already gravely endangered aspects of cultural identity that remain morally defensible, life sustaining, and life enhancing ultimately for all.

The warning flags of cultural assimilation, if not cultural genocide, are always very quickly raised by my indigenous colleagues.

It is however with his second thesis that I find the greatest fascination. Petrella (2008, 48) wonders about liberation theology becoming the foundation for other disciplines. He names economics, law, sociology, political science, medical anthropology as examples of the disciplines, which, "set the intellectual frameworks through which the world is most influentially analysed." He wonders aloud about subversively repositioning liberation theology as a transformative paradigm operating from within these now dominant academic disciplines in order to disrupt their prevailing presuppositions all of which he quite correctly claims, operate in favor of the wealthy.

I agree, but for me there is need for a prior step, and I think it is that the *educational blueprint underlying any and all intellectual frameworks including that of liberation theology that first requires radical developmental and transformative attention.*

I believe this means that liberation theology, *as an educational instrument—its curriculum, pedagogy, ideological, and political presuppositions and assessments,* must all first be reopened to critical interrogation. And not just liberation theology but in fact all of theology.

I say this because this our beloved academic discipline as least as I have experienced it over the past 20 years nationally, internationally, and ecumenically is still irrefutably so deeply mired in and by its colonial roots, still so inexorably fixated to and by its North Atlantic patronage. Unless and until the institutional infrastructure itself is transformed then all is rhetorical and the poor stay just that.

Let me offer an analogy by way of illustrating what I am driving at here. As with my brother Petrella, I too have long admired the astute observations of medical anthropologist Paul Farmer. Farmer is bold to claim "that as long as there is no even or equitable access to and benefit from health and human rights for all in God's world then what we will continue to bear witness to is diseases themselves making a preferential option for the poor" (2003, 140).

So too then do I suggest that in a perfectly analogous way that as long as there is no even or equitable access to, provision of and benefit from quality culturally sensitive and just theological education provision for all in God's world then what we will continue to bear witness to is academic insufficiency continuing to manifest itself within the theological academy as the 'preferential option for the poor' ... as it just did in the seminary for all of those beloved forefathers of mine all those years ago, just as continues to happen to women of color, to third world students, to those considered somewhat freakish for whatever reason.

The theological academy itself must first be radically transformed if its teaching of theology is to be instrumental in transforming the material conditions that give rise to poverty. The theological academy itself must be radically attuned to the self-interested politics of education that when unexamined for racial, gender, and class bias inevitably create and sustain institutional inequity.

If liberation theology is then to continue with broad based universal credibility to stake its claim to being premised on an unequivocal preferential option for the poor, then the challenge to ensure its own epistemological and pedagogical biases are in culturally authentic order is surely unavoidable.

Notes

1. See Boff and Boff (1986), Boff (1989), Bonino (1983), Knight (2003), Segundo (1976), and Sobrino (2008).
2. See his chapter in this book.

Bibliography

Boff, C., and L. Boff. 1986. *Introducing Liberation Theology*. Maryknoll: Orbis Books.

Boff, L. 1989. *The Maternal Face of God. The Feminine and Its Religious Expressions*. London: Collins.

Bonino, J. M. 1983. *Toward a Christian Political Ethic.* Minneapolis: Augsburg Fortress.

Farmer, P. 2003. *Pathologies of Power: Health, Human Rights and the New War on the Poor.* Berkeley: University of California Press.

Knight, W. F., ed. 2003. *An Account, Much Abbreviated, of the Destruction of the Indies, with Related Text.* Translated by A. Hurley. Minneapolis: Hackett.

Petrella, I. 2008. *Beyond Liberation Theology: A Polemic.* London: SCM.

Segundo, J. L. 1976. *The Liberation of Theology.* Maryknoll: Orbis Books.

Sobrino, J. 2008. *No Salvation Outside the Poor, Prophetic-Utopian Essays.* Maryknoll: Orbis Books.

CHAPTER 15

The Practice of Liberation Theology in the Twenty-First Century

Ivan Petrella

ipetrella@yahoo.com

I want to think about liberation theology without the constraints of the Christian tradition and theology generally. Of course, such an approach might bring immediate cries of warning: Didn't liberation theology spring from within Christianity? Is it not, as liberation theologians usually argue, the way the Christian tradition should be understood?

The answer to both questions, of course, is yes. But I want to take seriously the paradox that Marcella Althaus-Reid (2004, 79) noted at the heart of all liberationist Christian thinking: "The main task of liberationists has been to remove Christian passivity and attitudes of resignation which were precisely brought to our people's lives by centuries of Christian theology." Rarely has such a brutally honest statement been uttered and yet as far as I know it has been ignored.

This honest assessment is why she did not want to just reinterpret traditional Christian patriarchical structures. Doing so was "cosmetic surgery . . . putting new patches on old wineskins" (Althaus-Reid 2004, 74). The point, instead, was to create new ideas and institutions that required looking beyond traditional Christian resources.

We need, however, to go one better. We need to start to think about liberation theology outside of the limitations posed by theology itself. Today I want to suggest that key parts of liberation theology actually invite us to leave theology behind.

Are this is best, right?

The Heart of Liberation Theology: Three Elements

The first is epistemological, the liberationist attempt to do theology from the standpoint of the oppressed. Liberation theologies—whether Latin American, Black, womanist, feminist, queer, or others—realize that theology has traditionally been done from a standpoint of privilege. North Atlantic theology, like the distribution of global resources, is slanted toward the affluent, the male, the white, and the heterosexual; it is the product of a minority of humankind living in a state of affluent exception and enjoying gender, sexual, and racial dominance. Liberation theologies, instead, ground their thinking and practice in the perspective of the poor.

The second element is practical/moral: liberation theology's commitment to thinking about ideals by thinking about institutions. Early on liberation theologians realized that central categories such as "reign of god," "justice," or even "liberation" itself remain empty unless they are developed and given political and economic content. When Emilie Townes, for example, writes, "What is the society we are trying to create? What does it look like?...Any discussion that does not keep these questions in mind easily degenerates to theory and prospect rather than a blueprint for justice," she is highlighting the need to think about ideals in terms of institutions (2002, 89).

The third element is metaphysical, the belief that the modern world is not secular; it is idolatrous because the world is governed by ways of thinking that justify human sacrifices. So Larry Summers, when chief economist of the World Bank, could argue for the dumping of the world's most polluting industries in the poorest nations (George and Sabelli 1994, Chapter 5). How so? The poor consume and produce less so their contribution to the world economy is smaller than that of wealthier people. Their untimely death affects the global economy less. So if we are looking to set up industries that might cause untimely death, wherever the poor are, that is the place to do it.

Stepping Beyond Theology

Each element takes us beyond the way theology is usually thought about and practiced.

The epistemological: economics, law, political science, and a host of other disciplines could engage in the same shift with revolutionary consequences for each field. These are the disciplines, not theology, that set the frameworks through which the world is most influentially analyzed.

Liberation theology's epistemological shift needs to be transferred to disciplines with a wider impact than theology. Deep knowledge of those disciplines is required.

The practical/moral: the commitment to thinking about ideals by thinking about institutions is not an appendix to theology—it is part of liberation theology itself. For liberation theology, working the construction of political, economic, and social alternatives to the status quo is not a secondary moment in the theological task—coming after we have clarified our theological concepts—but rather it is the very means by which those concepts are given a degree of analytical rigor, clarified, and understood. You cannot do that without training in political economy, sociology, and law.

The metaphysical: the most dangerous idols, those that affect the greatest number of people, are not found in the traditional religious sphere but outside of it. They are found in the supposedly secular realm. Theological critique, therefore, is now directed toward uncovering the idolatrous theologies that lurk within the social sciences. Expertise in those disciplines is key.

Rethinking Theological Education and Theologians

Theological Education

At a time when some seminaries are making bold moves, Claremont, for example, and its multireligious approach, bold moves are required here as well. If we grant this understanding of liberation theology, the understanding I have developed, we need to realize that the very content of what is taught and transmitted in seminaries and divinity schools fails to prepare students for the interdisciplinary nature of their vocation.

Notice that I said that seminaries often fail to prepare students for the interdisciplinary nature of their vocation. Let me stress that I do not mean profession, I mean vocation. One's profession may be that of a professor or a pastor. But one's vocation is to transform lives and society.

There is no necessary link between being a professor or pastor and the vocation of transformation. What do we want to shape and train? Do we want to train for a profession or do we want to train for a vocation? The vocation to transform in light of our understanding of what is right and just?

If so, liberation theology's three key elements require a much deeper grounding in disciplines that are often not taught enough. Students need ample training in economics, political science, sociology, law, medical anthropology, and other disciplines. Of course, one person cannot encompass all these fields. But a student must be in close conversation with at least a number of them. At least a year-long course that examines different social theories from a liberationist bent should be developed and required, and doctoral students should have an allied field where they should be able to hold their own theology and law, or theology and economics, or others.

Otherwise how can you transfer liberation theology's epistemological shift to other disciplines where it is urgently necessary? Otherwise how can you develop concrete visions of society that give content to our theological ideals such as liberation? Otherwise how can you recognize the idolatry lurking within other disciplines?

If we want to remain faithful to our vocation, a transformation of theological education is required.

The Theologian

What does this mean for the way we understand the theologian? Leonardo and Clodovis Boff (1987), in their *Introducing Liberation Theology* describe three types of liberation theologians: popular, pastoral, and professional. I would like to add a fourth, the undercover liberation theologian.

The undercover liberation theologian separates the vocation from the profession. He or she goes undercover in another discipline and works from within to transform its presuppositions and practice. Paul Farmer is an example within medical anthropology. He explicitly rethinks his discipline in light of the preferential option for the poor. He is an example of the transformative power of combining liberation theology with medical anthropology.

Sergio Fajardo, former mayor of Medellín Colombia, provides another. In 2004 Fajardo became mayor of Medellín, the most violent city in Latin America. In that year Medellín had suffered 6,300 homicides. In his last year as mayor, the city suffered 771 homicides. Victims of violent crime are inordinately the poor. This is a major transformation. How did he pull it off? Usually governments do not focus much on the poorest parts of their city. They might build a school or a health center and take years to do so.

Instead, Fajardo sought to break the idea that the poor are an afterthought. He tackled Medellín with a large-scale urban plan. The goal: to touch every fiber of a community's being. People had to feel like something radical was changing in their lives and their surroundings. So his government did not take years to build a school. He built Medellín's best and most beautiful schools in the poorest parts of the city. But not just schools. Some of the best health centers, libraries, cultural and scientific centers, and botanical gardens are now in the city's poorest neighborhoods. And all of these include programs directed toward children.

Forty-five percent of the city's budget was spent on education widely conceived as the revamping of public space and the rearticulation of a city with its poor. Why spend that money? To highlight a person's dignity no matter what their social standing. When the poorest people say, "the most beautiful things are here, where I live," they see that their children can have a future.

His architecture and urban planning motto: "The most beautiful things, for the poorest people" (Alcaldia de Medellín 2008). Fajardo's statement brings out the best of liberation theology and urban planning. Again, "the most beautiful things, for the poorest people."

It is a tremendously powerful statement that in his hands made of architecture an undercover liberation theology. A liberation theology of bricks and mortar and parks and schools.

"The most beautiful things, for the poorest people."

Let us find ways to forge links like this in the future, or educate those younger than us so they may accomplish what today we cannot.

Bibliography

Alcaldia de Medellín. 2008. *Del Miedo a la Esperanza: Alcaldia de Medellín 2004–2007*. Medellín: Alcaldia de Medellín.

Althaus-Reid, M. 2004. *From Feminist Theology to Indecent Theology*. London: SCM.

Boff, L., and C. Boff. 1987. *Introducing Liberation Theology*. Maryknoll: Orbis.

Farmer, P. 2003. *Pathologies of Power: Health, Human Rights, and the New War on the Poor*. Berkeley: University of California Press.

George, S., and F. Sabelli. 1994. *Faith and Credit: The World Bank's Secular Empire*. Bounder: Westview.

Townes, E. 2002. "Living in the New Jerusalem: The Rhetoric and Movement of Liberation in the House of Evil." In *A Troubling in My Soul: Womanist Perspectives on Evil and Suffering*, ed. E. M. Townes, 78–91. Maryknoll: Orbis Books.

PART V

Future

CHAPTER 16

Popular Messianism, Complicity, and the Continued Relevance of Liberation Theology

Jeremy Ian Kirk
kirkjeremy@me.com

At the end of 2009, James Cameron released the film *Avatar*, which would become the highest grossing film in history. Four weeks prior, at the annual meeting of the American Academy of Religion, representatives of the religious academy celebrated the fortieth anniversary of James Cone's *Black Theology & Black Power* by granting him the Martin Marty award for the Public Understanding of Religion. The film *Avatar* and the work of Cone share a common call for liberation. Both are concerned with the material and historical liberation of persons subject to particular instances of systemically enforced suffering.[1] In addition, both Cameron and Cone's projects are theological. They both locate God(dess) as existing among oppressed peoples, suffering with them and siding with them in fighting against their oppressors and for their liberation.

Despite these similarities, the liberation in *Avatar* (an example *par excellence* of contemporary popular messianism) is not like the liberation found in black liberation theology. They are opposed to one another to such an extent that the messianic in *Avatar* is the anti-Christ of black liberation theology. I will examine how *Avatar* deals with conversion and solidarity on the part of the human protagonist, Jake Sully, who turns against the human colonial forces by fighting alongside the indigenous population for their liberation. Finally, I will redirect my critique of Cameron toward the liberal religious academy and argue for renewed engagement with liberative projects on the part of my generation of scholars that seek to address the relationship between our scholarship and particular cases of systemic oppression. The final portion of this essay will propose next steps toward the formation of a liberative social ethic for those who identify themselves as complicit in the systemic injustices they purport to resist.

The Messianic in Black Liberation Theology and in *Avatar*

A Black Christology of Liberation

Fueled by his outrage over the dehumanization of black people in the United States, Cone cited (1997a, vii), "*liberation* as the heart of the Christian gospel and *blackness* as the primary mode of God's presence." Cone admonished white theologians for not addressing racism and sought to construct a black theology that placed at its center God's affirmation of black personhood and the biblical mandate for the material liberation of black people suffering under white supremacy.[2]

For Cone, salvation is located in God's identity as an oppressed person through Jesus of Nazareth. Cone expresses this through the theological claim that Jesus is black. He argues for Jesus' blackness by correlating the historical material circumstances of black people in the United States to those of Jews under Roman rule and throughout the history of Israel's oppression. He explains that "the blackness of God means that God has made the oppressed condition God's own condition" (Cone 1990, 63) and therefore is present with oppressed people in their suffering.

For Cone (1997b 124), the cross of Jesus represents how fully God chooses to identify with oppressed peoples. He states:

> The theological significance of the cross and resurrection is what makes the life of Jesus more than just the life of a good man who happened to like the poor. *The finality of Jesus lies in the totality of his existence in complete freedom as the Oppressed One who reveals through his death and resurrection that God is present in all dimensions of human liberation.* His death is the revelation of the freedom of God, taking upon himself the totality of human oppression; his resurrection is the disclosure that God is not defeated by oppression but transforms it into the possibility of freedom. (1990, 18)

To better understand the relevance of this hopeful message of the cross to the material needs of oppressed people, we must examine precisely what Cone perceives happens on the cross. Cone points to what Reinhold Niebuhr describes as "the terrible beauty of the cross"[3] as well as Niebuhr's (1937, Chapter 10) explanation of God's victory on the cross as a "transvaluation of values."

Appropriating the phrase from Frederick Nietzsche, Niebuhr uses "transvaluation of values" to show how God's apparent defeat, seen in Jesus's weakness on the Cross, actually functions as the ultimate condemnation of human power and hubris (Niebuhr 1941, 186), and thereby reveals God's judgment over sinful humanity through a reversal of human values. Quoting Niebuhr periodically, Cone explains:

> "The crucified messiah [is] the final revelation of the divine character and divine purpose." He was rejected because people expected a Messiah "perfect in power and perfect in goodness." But "the revelation of divine goodness in history must be powerless; thus God's revelation transvalues human values, turning them upside down. If human power in history—among races, nations and other collectives as well as individuals—is *self-interested power*, then "the revelation of divine goodness in history" must be weak and not strong. "The Christ is led as the lamb to the slaughter." Human values focus on self-interest, which no individual or group can completely escape. Thus from a human standpoint, the Messiah must not suffer but must overcome suffering with power. (2011, Chapter 2)

The cross is salvific, but salvation comes amidst defeat, horror, and the suffering of the innocent. These and other theologies of the cross bring hope to victims of oppression because they place the suffering of human beings at the center of God's concerns for and activity in the world.

Avatar's White Messiah and *Deus Ex Machina*

In *Avatar*, the messianic is comprised of three related characters: Sully, the goddess Eywa, and the indigenous warrior Tsu'tey. Sully, a disabled Marine veteran, turned mercenary, turned anticolonial revolutionary, plays the role of the deliverer-prophet of the oppressed indigenous population. The goddess Eywa, the object of the indigenous population's monotheistic and panentheistic religious faith, represents divine power and justice siding with the oppressed. Finally, Tsu'tey, lead warrior of the local indigenous clan, plays a sacrificial role.

Sully, played by Sam Worthington,[4] joins a corporate colonial space-mission to mine the distant planet of Pandora. Sully is a security member of a science team tasked with studying and communicating with the indigenous population called the Na'vi in order to convince them to peacefully allow the corporate colonial force to mine their land. The science team operates through cloned Na'vi bodies, which they inhabit remotely, but grant their operators the vantage point and physical abilities of a Na'vi. In the course of his work infiltrating a local Na'vi clan, Sully is seduced by the Na'vi way of life and falls in love with a Na'vi princess named Neytiri, played by Zoe Saldana. He subsequently joins the Na'vi resistance and leads them in a battle for liberation against the human colonial military force (Cameron 2010b).

The film's narrative portrays Sully as becoming one of the Na'vi people through a brief immersion in which he learns their language, culture, spirituality, and their special relationship to nature including their ability to "bond" (Cameron 2010b, disk 1, 00:59:24) with and ride large dragon-like creatures that the humans call "banshees." Sully is named "one of the people" by the Na'vi clan in a cultural/religious ceremony (Cameron 2010b, disk 1, 01:21:18). The film tries to justify his conversion from colonial oppressor to indigenous warrior and eventually leader of the clan.[5] But the film's attempt fails. Sully hides his true identity and purpose (as colonial agent) from the Na'vi people.[6] He may look like them, act like them, and share some recent experiences with them, but he does not share their history. He has not suffered with them and therefore does not share their ontology or communal and cultural identity. Furthermore, while Sully does consistently take risks, he is always doing so with a reward on the horizon: a reconnection to nature, love and sex with Neytiri,[7] the ability to fly, and most of all acceptance by and absolution from those in whose oppression he has participated. The goddess Eywa chooses Sully to assume the most venerated role in Na'vi culture and history: Toruk Macto, the traditional messianic warrior of Na'vi folklore.[8] In assuming this role, Sully replaces Tsu'tey, played by Laz Alanso,[9] as the paradigmatic Na'vi clan warrior.

Tsu'tey, the head warrior and successor to the clan chief, primarily represents the sacrificial aspect of *Avatar*'s messianic narrative.[10] He is the suffering servant of the Na'vi clan. Unlike Sully, he is actually Na'vi and resists human colonization from a place of deep cultural love and identity. Tsu'tey suffers, first in his experience as one who is being colonized, and second in sacrificing his life in battle for the liberation of his people from colonial oppression. Unfortunately, Tsu'tey's character primarily serves to support the narrative of Sully's acceptance into the clan. Tsu'tey is the hardest to convince of Sully's belonging, especially after Sully steals Neytiri, his betrothed. But by the end of the film, Tsu'tey has repeatedly endorsed Sully's leadership thereby absolving the oppressor who changes sides (if nothing else).

Just before his death, Tsu'tey's final words venerate Sully in exclaiming that the totality of his life's meaning can be encompassed in the knowledge that he fought with Sully, Toruk Macto (Cameron 2010b, disk 01:10:29).[11]

The third, and final piece of *Avatar*'s messianic trinity, is the goddess Eywa who at a critical moment in the battle with the colonial military, releases the full force of the jungle creatures upon the colonial military, decimating their forces and thus saving the day (Cameron 2010b, disk 2, 00:57:20). This act establishes Eywa as the *deus ex machina*, the god(dess) who swoops in at the last possible moment to save the day by way of a previously unexplained mechanism. Previously in the film, when Sully prays for Eywa's help in defeating the colonial forces, Neytiri warns Sully that Eywa does not take sides (Cameron 2010b, disk 2, 00:45:50). Upon realizing that Eywa had saved the day, Neytiri exclaims to Sully that Eywa heard his prayer, thus further elevating Sully among the Na'vi as a spiritual, as well as military, leader.

Avatar's Messiah as Black Liberation Theology's Antichrist

The fact that the highest grossing movie of all time can incorporate an explicitly liberationist, anticolonial, and pro-ecological narrative may indicate progress since Cone published *Black Theology and Black Power* in 1969, but the details of the film's narrative show how far we still have to go. *Avatar*'s messiah exemplifies black liberation theology's antichrist, albeit one particular to contemporary liberalism. Cameron's messiah lacks the defining characteristics of black liberation theology's messiah and in some cases bears opposite characteristics.

Avatar's messiah, in all three of its iterations, fails to serve oppressed peoples' needs for liberation. Sully is a white, colonial messiah. He cannot liberate the Na'vi people because he is not one of them. His leadership is the leadership of the righteous ally-oppressor whose noble actions of solidarity, paired with the powers of the *deus ex machina*, save the Na'vi in the short term but do not liberate them. The Na'vi have no self-determination but rather fight only symbolically. Furthermore, unlike the critical role weakness plays in the liberationist Christologies of Cone and others, there is no room for weakness in *Avatar*'s messiah. Weakness is relegated to the sacrifice of Tsu'tey whose suffering plays virtually no role in the victory over the colonial military. While the film attempts to highlight human and ecological frailty, especially through Sully's disability as a paraplegic, all frailty in *Avatar* is overcome and discarded; Sully gets "resurrected"[12] permanently as an able-bodied

Na'vi and Eywa clearly has the power to recover from the ecological wounds caused by the humans.

The film also consistently associates heroism with masculine dominance. Two examples of this are Sully's dominance of Tsu'tey, in which he replaces Tsu'tey as clan leader and mate to Neytiri, as well as his dominance of the indigenous people's culture and religion through assuming their most sacred role of Toruk Macto. A third and more explicit example of male dominance is Sully dominating his banshee during their initial "bonding" (Cameron 2010b, disk 1, 01:19:30). Neytiri describes the bonding of a Na'vi to a banshee as a mutual choosing and thus a consensual and collaborative act (Cameron 2010b, disk 1, 0:61:06). Contrary to this description, Sully violently coerces his banshee into bonding with him.[13] First, he silences the creature's voice by muzzling it with a rope. He then mounts and straddles the dragon-like beast before forcing it to bond with him.[14] After he breaks the creature into submission, Sully grabs its muzzle, looks into its fearful eye and declares triumphantly, "That's right...you're mine" (Cameron 2010b, disk 1, 01:22:11). Sully's power is defined over and against nature in a way that more closely resembles sexual assault than a mutual bonding between human(oid) and nature.

In the film, Cameron's protagonist never changes, though he does switch sides. The tools of oppression are simply reordered to counter oppression through the agency of the oppressor-turned-ally. There is no *transvaluation of values* but only an appropriation of militant colonial values for the sake of the oppressed indigenous population. This produces a positive historical-material result for the Na'vi in the short term but does not ultimately liberate them because they have played such a minor role in their own revolution.[15]

Whose needs do *Avatar*'s narrative serve if not the Na'vi? The narrative serves Sully's needs; Cameron's needs; my needs; the needs of educated white liberals who despite our best intentions of solidarity center our own crises of complicity and need for absolution in our discourses on liberation and social justice. Cameron has described his film as a pro-ecological, anti-imperialist, and anticapitalist project, and he has used the film's success to raise awareness and attempt to affect policy surrounding the Belo Monte dam project in Brazil, which threatens the lives and culture of indigenous Brazilians.[16] While this work is certainly admirable, Cameron's film has nothing to offer to oppressed people or to those of us who, like Cameron, seek to resist oppressive systems from which we also benefit materially.

Getting Solidarity Right: Toward a Liberative Social Ethic for the Complicit

Privileged people who claim to be affecting progressive social change need to get solidarity right.[17] Cone (1997a 150–52) explains that for whites to reconcile with their victims and thus with God, they must become black. Unlike the mere aesthetic trick played by *Avatar*'s protagonist, "becoming black" for privileged scholars today requires an interrogation of and confrontation with our academic guild's complicity in the perpetuation of systemic oppression. Like Cameron, in responding to the horror of our complicity, we often take up projects that serve our own existential crises of guilt rather than the root crisis of human material suffering under systemic injustice.[18] To correct this, we must actively work to recenter the people who suffer materially under systemic injustice as those to whom the historical effects of our work are accountable.

One way in which I hope to contribute to these ends is by constructing a liberationist social ethic for the complicit. This project asks the following two questions: (1) What is the significance of resisting systemic injustice as people who occupy social locations that benefit materially from the injustices we purport to resist? and (2), how do we work effectively toward the increased material well-being of people who suffer under systemic injustice?

Such a liberative social ethic of the complicit must work toward an understanding of what it means to be complicit allies. First, this will involve telling our own stories of wrestling with complicity and listening to the stories of others.[19] Similar attempts in the past have been stunted at the level of confession, but we must move beyond this in order to enact substantive historical material change. Second, in order to be effective, any contemporary liberationist project must take seriously and address recent criticisms leveled against liberation theology. This will require serious analyses of identity and power, especially the role of class in instances of contemporary oppression and in light of an increasingly globalized capitalist world, and how liberationist projects will take into account instances in which particular representatives of historically marginalized groups now hold positions of great social power. Third, a liberative Christian social ethic for the complicit must include a Christology for the complicit, which seeks to reconcile our images of Jesus with those revealed through the lived experiences of our sisters and brothers who have suffered under the systemic oppressions we seek to resist. Fourth, and most importantly, in order to determine an appropriate praxis of complicit-allyhood, which prioritizes the liberation of those in whose suffering we are complicit rather than prioritize our own exoneration from complicity, we must enter into active relationship with those on whose behalf we would act, allowing for those relationships to direct our discernment and action.

Let me conclude with one concrete example. In my own experience, the framework of so-called ontological blackness has been very useful for interrogating complicity in and responsibility for systemic injustices. As long as people's material wellbeing can be determined by their social categorization, that social categorization must be addressed, critically engaged, and at times re-appropriated for the cause of liberation. Thus the categories of both blackness and whiteness continue to be areas of important intellectual engagement.

However, the critical framework of ontological blackness may not, in all cases, be the most effective framework for mobilizing the would-be complicit-allies of oppressed people to actually work toward substantive social change. This framework may in certain instances obscure the potential unity among lower social classes of plural cultural or perceived ethnic differences. Thus we need to imagine other models in cooperation with the aims of ontological blackness.

One such cooperative model can be found in the ontologizing of hope proposed by philosopher Ernst Bloch. He (1986, 65) posited that human "anticipatory consciousness," or the ability to conceive of a potential future that improves upon the oppressive conditions of the past and present, is more than just a mindset but is rather a state of being, as this consciousness of what he calls the "not yet" (1986, 75) continually constructs our self-understanding and action in history. Thus we are not so much static beings but are constantly "becoming" and "in-process" toward an uncertain, yet hoped-for, future (Bloch 1986, 209).

Entertaining this materialist ontology of hope and liberation seems to open space for further envisioning of the liberative praxiological role of those who identify as complicit in the systemic injustices they purport to resist. It does this by inviting them to join in the present stream of the potential future reconciled society. This parallels what Cone refers to "becoming black" but also accounts for complex and multiple identities of the people who identify as complicit as well as the complex structures of power and oppression often evoked in critiquing ontological blackness and identity politics in general. Such a model also emphasizes class analysis without negating the importance of identity categories based on social constructions of race, gender, sexuality, and ability. Such a model may help contribute to the growth and unity of what is increasingly being referred to as the 99 percent.

Notes

1. I use the phrase "enforced suffering," from Aloysius Pieris, SJ, as a more descriptive synonym for "oppression." See Pieris (1988).
2. See Dorrien (2008).
3. See Cone (2011, Chapter 2) and Niebuhr (1929, 386). Cone notes that Niebuhr may have borrowed the phrase "terrible beauty" from Yeats (1994, 194–196).
4. Sam Worthington is Caucasian. A deeper analysis of race in *Avatar* (Cameron 2010b) could explore the significance of this white man inhabiting a blue indigenous body.
5. Jake's leadership of the clan is made explicit in the Collector's Extended Cut. See ibid., disk 2, 01:09:53.
6. The film addresses his dishonesty and he is temporarily named as not "one of the people," though this is quickly changed when he assumes the role of Toruk Macto. See ibid., disk 2, 00:13:00.
7. A feminist critique of the film could address the fact that the entire aesthetic of the Na'vi people was designed around the need for Neytiri to be sexually appealing to Jake as well as to the audience of the film.
8. This choosing by Eywa is implicit throughout the film. Later in prayer, Jake explicitly identifies himself as chosen by Eywa. See Cameron (2010b), disk 2, 00:44:47.
9. This actor is African American. He is only depicted through the virtual Na'vi "makeup" digitally imposed onto his body. However, his features still communicate his "blackness" to many viewers. A deeper analysis of race in the film could explore how actors chosen to play Na'vi characters still communicate Western racial categories .
10. It could be argued that the human character Trudy Chacon, played by Michelle Rodriguez, also fills this sacrificial role. As a human ally to the Na'vi she is a better exemplar of liberationist solidarity than Jake because she gives her life on behalf of Na'vi liberation with apparently little outside motivation. David Horstkoetter makes a similar observation. See Horstkoetter (2010).
11. Much to the dismay of the director and many others who worked on this film, this fully rendered scene was cut from the theatrical version of the film to save time. It was included in all post theatrical releases of the film.
12. Despite never having to die.
13. "Banshee" refers specifically to a female spirit from Irish folklore.
14. The appendages used to bond evoke both phallic and vaginal imagery.
15. Cone argues that the true liberation of the oppressed can only come from oppressed people themselves and states that black theology "assumes that the possibilities of creative response among white people to black humiliation are virtually nonexistent. What slim possibilities there are belong only to those whites who are wholly committed to the activity of destroying

racism in the structure of the white community." In light of Cone's statement, it can be said that in *Avatar*, Jake fights *whites* but not *whiteness*. See, Cone (1997a, 117–18).

16. See Democracy Now! (2010).

17. I employ two terms I have yet to come to peace with. The first is "solidarity," which has been rightly problematized by many scholars. The second term is "ally." I am more comfortable with the use of this term because it has been bestowed upon me by LGBTQI persons, some of whom call me an "ally" to communicate their acceptance of my intent to promote their material wellbeing and social liberation.

18. This is evidenced by the way in which criticism of liberation theologies in the academy has seemingly functioned to dismiss liberationist discourse, rather than function as necessary constructive-critical components of improved liberationist projects.

19. The prompting of Professor Ada María Isasi-Díaz and my seminary colleague Amy Barbour inspired this addition. This should not be confused with an attempt to center the stories of the complicit-allies in a larger conversation about human liberation, but rather as a necessary step in determining whom we are so we can then discern how we should respond as a particular portion of larger cooperative response to oppression.

Bibliography

Bloch, E. 1986. *The Principle of Hope*. 1st ed. Studies in contemporary German social thought. Cambridge: MIT Press.

Cameron, J. 2010a. *Avatar* (Three-Disk Extended Collector's Edition). DVD. Twentieth Century Fox.

————. 2010b. *Avatar: Collector's Extended Cut*. DVD. Twentieth Century Fox.

Cone, J. H. 1990. *A Black Theology of Liberation*. 20th ed. Maryknoll: Orbis Books.

————. 1997a. *Black Theology and Black Power*. Maryknoll: Orbis Books.

————. 1997b. *God of the Oppressed*. Rev Sub. Maryknoll: Orbis Books.

————. 2011. *The Cross and the Lynching Tree*. Maryknoll: Orbis Books.

Democracy Now! 2010. "'Avatar' Director James Cameron Follows Box Office Success with Advocacy for Indigenous Struggles." April 27. http://www.democracynow.org/2010/4/27/avatar_director_james_cameron_follows_box.

Dorrien, G. J. 2008. *Social Ethics in the Making: Interpreting an American Tradition*. Malden: Blackwell.

Horstkoetter, D. 2010. "'Everyone in This Room is Now Dumber for Having Listened to [Him]' : Setting Straight the Insanity of Glenn Beck on James Cone and Black Liberation Theology." *The Other Journal* 17 (July 22). http://www.theotherjournal.com/?s=everyone+in+the+room+is+now+dumber.

Niebuhr, R. 1929. "The Terrible Beauty of the Cross." *The Christian Century*, March 21.

————. 1937. *Beyond Tragedy: Essays on the Christian Interpretation of History*. New York: C. Scribner's.

———. 1941. *The Nature and Destiny of Man: A Christian Interpretation*. Gifford lectures 1939. New York: C. Scribner's.

Pieris, A. 1988. *An Asian Theology of Liberation*. Maryknoll: Orbis Books.

Yeats, W. B. 1994. "Easter, 1916." In *Holy Fire*, ed. Dan Halpern. New York: Harper Perennial.

CHAPTER 17

Toward a Twenty-First Century Black Liberation Ethic: A Marxist Reclamation of Ontological Blackness

Charlene Sinclair
charlenesinclair@gmail.com

In *Beyond Ontological Blackness,* Victor Anderson critiques Black theology as a theo-intellectual project whose ontological claims of blackness requires white racism and black crisis. Anderson asserts:

> In black theology, blackness has become a totality of meaning. It cannot point to any transcendent meaning beyond itself without also fragmenting. Because black life is fundamentally determined by black suffering and resistance to whiteness (the power of non-being), black existence is without the possibility of transcendence from the blackness that whiteness created. (1995, 91–92)

In other words Black theology's reinforcing dualism of white racism and black survival is an "iron cage" that James Cone, not society, created. In addition, this iron cage, which "justifies itself as radically oppositional to whiteness, nevertheless requires whiteness, white racism, and white theology for the self-disclosure of its new black being and its legitimacy" (Anderson 1995, 91–92).

Although Black theology places at the center a demand for the recognition of the humanity of black people at the margins and has thus led to various theologies of recognition, when read through a Marxist lens, Cone's call for ontological blackness emerges as more than merely a theological project of black recognition of self, suffering, and survival. As Cone (1990, 7) indicates, "The focus on blackness does not mean that only blacks suffer as victims in a racist society, but that blackness is an ontological symbol and a visible reality which best describes what oppression means in America."

In Cone's schema, whiteness is not the requirement for a black understanding of self; rather Cone calls us to reject the role a construction termed whiteness plays in the oppression and social control of the other. For Cone this process of rejection begins with casting off whiteness and taking on the other. Black theology in its defining of Black power as "a humanizing force" attempts to construct a theological basis for the disruption of the dehumanizing force of white supremacy—it is a counter-hegemonic move that says no to the oppressive hegemonic dominion of capitalism over and against those at the bottom; a bottom that is disproportionately filled with brothers and sisters of a darker hue.

Cone brings a powerful message that peeks through but has not been fully apprehended. Blackness as a sociopolitical symbol is more than what has been done to a particular people; it is indicative of how a society has structured misery, power, ideological hegemony, and social control. Hence, blackness gives us more than a clue to the marginalized people in the United States; if probed deeply, it reveals the infrastructure that supports the alienating oppression of those at the bottom, irrespective of color, irrespective of place. Once this infrastructure previously hidden by the cloak of melanin is revealed, structural transformation, not merely recognition, becomes the imperative. This is a move that Anderson overlooks in his attempt to move beyond ontological blackness.

This move becomes more visible when placed into dialogue with Marx's critique of political economy. Though often reduced to a theorist concerned only with economic relations, class struggles, and the control of the means of production, Marx's analyses have much wider implications and are deeply concerned with the analysis and disruption of oppressive and alienating social relations. For Marx (1976, 178) "*economic categories* are only *abstract expressions* of actual human relations."

In addition, Marx argues that there is a circular reinforcing interrelationship between human production and societal formation: it is an eternal ever-evolving loop. Human beings in their productive engagement with their environment shape the social and political structures of their world, at the same time the social and political structures of society shape the lives of individuals. In other words, we are always circumscribed to the reality we find ourselves in even as we (re)create that reality. Therefore the determination of who we are (or think we are), how we view ourselves and society, and not merely what is produced, are the results of productive processes (Marx 1976, 180). Thus a thorough-going analysis of society must begin with an analysis of production and its role in the creation of human social relationships.

Central to Marx's analysis is the unmasking of the oppressive and alienating forces of capitalist processes that distort human relationships and human flourishing. In *Capital,* Marx utilizes the liberal illusion of a utopian "inside Eden" movement of capital as an almost tongue in cheek explication of capitalism. For Marx, inside Eden is where the *complete equality* between the owner of money and the owner of labor power is assumed. It is where the free noncoerced entrance and exchange of commodity occurs.

However, this Eden does not account for the lack of equality that actually shapes the exchange of money for labor power. Outside of Eden where the real exchange of money for labor happens, we do not find a mutually advantageous process. Rather, within this process is an unequal exchange where labor power is on the market as a commodity and the possessor of labor power is compelled to "offer for sale as a commodity that very labour-power which exists in his living body" (Marx 1992, 272).

Marx then juxtaposes this inside Eden movement of capital against the reality of people's history and experience to show the destructive alienating and exploitive nature of capitalism, monopoly, and greed when allowed unrestricted movement in the quest for profit. Alienation therefore is the process by which human labor as commodity becomes a thing that is bought and sold rather than "a unique source of personal identity" (McNally 2006, 65). Control of this labor upon purchase rests with the purchaser, not with laborer herself. Having no control over what is produced, how it is produced, or on the profits of the production, the laborer becomes alienated from their labor and from their very selves. However, the capitalist now in control of the labor sets the terms and is able to determine the value of labor via wages. The "difference between labor's output and the wages paid—called surplus value—is the secret to the massive inequalities of capitalism" (McNally 2006, 65).

The polemic that Marx created was purposefully done to expose the liberal state and its pursuit of unrestricted private property accumulation as *unfree and unequal and unnatural.* According to Marx, liberal ideology is the ideology of unrestricted private property ownership wrapped in the illusory opiate of bourgeois human rights and the capitalist market, the illusory place where those rights are actualized. However, for Marx this alienation and exploitation also gives rise to mass misery and oppression. Marx (1992, 929) therefore posits that the result will be a "revolt of the working class...trained, united and organized by the mechanism of the capitalist process of production."

However, as Marx (1992, 414) has noted, "Labor cannot emancipate itself in the white skin where in the black it is branded." Inherent in the above analysis is a monolithic working class and an analysis of surplus value that has not fully emerged from within Eden. White Western liberal and Marxist analysis does not often acknowledge the utilization of race as a form of stratification within the working class. Stratification is used as a mechanism of social control thereby also producing intra-class antagonisms. In other words, workers do not automatically cohere into a monolithic working class without struggle. The failure to theorize the impact of race on social structures as well as social relations masks the distortions and stalls the development of a revolutionary class of workers.

Furthermore, operating outside of Eden, wage and surplus value hold an additional secret—the property of whiteness. Cheryl Harris (1993, 1713), author of "Whiteness as Property," states, "in ways so embedded that it is rarely apparent, the set of assumptions, privileges, and benefits that accompany the status of being white have become a valuable asset," an asset "protected by the law...even though the law is neither uniform nor explicit in all instances, in protecting settled expectations based on white privilege, American law has recognized a property interest in whiteness."

Thus outside of Eden, David Roediger (2007, 13) drawing on the work of W. E. B. DuBois asserts,

> Whiteness could function as a 'wage' for white workers. That is, status and privileges conferred by race could be used to make up for the alienating and exploitative class relationships, North and South. White workers could, and did, define and accept their class positions by fashioning identities as 'not slaves' and 'not blacks'. When they did so, Du Bois argued, the wages of whiteness often turned out to be spurious.

Therefore, if we accept Marx's theory of social relations embedded within and the resultant of production processes, then a US liberation enterprise would call for a thoroughgoing analysis of the impact of racialized propertied bodies on human relations at the inceptive core of US capitalism. Thus the centrality of an unapologetic appropriation of "blackness" in Cone's Black theology is the first step and serves as a corrective for a white Marxian analysis that ignores the historic role of blackness and the privileged "property-ing" of whiteness in the capitalist production process.

In its radical, jarring, disjunctive rejection of the system of oppression, ontological blackness seeks to break the stronghold that the symbols of oppression has on our social, economic political, and psychic being. Ontological blackness affirms that we are crafted in the image of God irrespective of the immense distortion of our very beings through the mechanism of capitalist social production. It acknowledges not only our alienation from each other but also our profound alienation from ourselves. Ontological blackness therefore becomes an unwavering confrontation with structures of oppression that have systematically created and sustained physical, social economic, political, and psychic alienation—human from human. It is a call for radical humanness.

Conclusion

We are all familiar with Marx's definition of religion as the "opium of the people" but many rarely hear the precursor to Marx's conclusion. According to Marx, "Religion is the sigh of the oppressed creature, the sentiment of a heartless world, and the soul of soulless conditions" (2002, 171). It is the failure of religion to resist the historical conditions of human misery and its propensity to project a kingdom outside of earth that Marx is railing against. For Marx,

> The abolition of religion as the illusory happiness of men, is a demand for their real happiness. The call to abandon their illusions about their condition is a call to abandon a condition which requires illusions . . . The criticism of religion disillusions man so that he will think, act and fashion his reality as a man who has lost his illusions and regained his reason (2002, 171).

Cone would agree with Marx that the historic conditions of misery must be resisted; however, in Marx's critique of religion, they part company. Cone argues that God is the God of liberation and we become reconciled through our taking up of blackness and confrontation with the very systems that produce this alienation. In the development of a Black theology of liberation, Cone understood that one of the most powerful organizing forces (as shown by Martin and quite frankly Malcolm) is not the factory but the places where people gather to express their deepest pain and their greatest hope. It is the place where the reality of life meets the possibility of a different world. It is in places of spiritual worship. However, we must ward against a transcendent spirituality that point to an otherworldly reality without engaging the pain of this world. Therefore in agreement with James Cone, I argue that race and its resulting child racism is so deeply embedded in Euro-American history and culture (social production) that it is impossible to do a theological ethic that is liberative without BEING black—impossible without a position of ontological blackness. Thus it is only in the engagement of race, and the dehumanizing misery that racialization and racism created, that a US liberationist ethic with claims to Christian roots can emerge.

It is in this endeavor that Cone's black ontology is a Marxian dialectic in its truest eschatological sense. It is a call for a dialectic that moves beyond an abstract formulaic equation of thesis + antithesis = synthesis. It is a negation that seeks human emancipation through its negation of a whiteness that separates and kills, an oppositional force that beckons us to say no to structures of oppression and alienation and yes to our reconciliation with each other and with God. A blackness that if taken up moves us toward a new and ever-emerging creation—a new world perhaps a step closer (albeit a baby step) toward the kin-dom of God.

Bibliography

Anderson, V. 1995. *Beyond Ontological Blackness: An Essay on African American Religious and Cultural Criticism.* New York: Continuum.

Cone, J. H. 1990. *A Black Theology of Liberation,* 20th anniversary ed.. Maryknoll: Orbis Books.

Harris, C. I., 1993. "Whiteness as Property." *Harvard Law Review* 106:8, 1707. http://papers.ssrn.com/sol3/papers.cfm?abstract_id=927850. Accessed February 14, 2012.

Marx, K., and F. Engels. 2002. "Critique on Hegel's Philosophy of Right." In *Marx on Religion,* ed. John Raines. Philadelphia: Temple University Press.

Marx, K. 1976. *The Poverty of Philosophy: Answer to the "Philosophy of Poverty" by M. Proudhon.* Toronto: Norman Bethune Institute.

———. 1992. *Capital: Volume 1: A Critique of Political Economy.* London: Penguin Classics.

McNally, D. 2006. *Another World Is Possible: Globalization and Anti-Capitalism.* Revised and updated. Winnipeg: Arbeiter Ring.

Roediger, D. R. 2007. *The Wages of Whiteness: Race and the Making of the American Working Class.* Revised and expanded. London: Verso.

CHAPTER 18

A Christian Liberationist Response to the Crisis at the United States– Mexico Border

William A. Walker III
william.walker@cgu.edu

In this paper I will discuss the problem of violence related to the US-Mexico drug trade as understood within the framework of political and economic globalization. This will require a brief overview of my political-theological method. I will then provide a liberationist theological reflection on the problem from a North American Christian perspective. In closing I will offer a short ethical analysis in light of this theological reasoning.[1]

From the perspective of theology as a discipline, the impetus for this essay is the concern that, while liberation theology as traditionally conceived has perhaps run its course, the usefulness of the tools given to political theologians by liberation theology can only be judged by their continuous applicability. In more concrete terms, therefore, the intention here is for the application of a liberationist hermeneutic to actually aid in the development of a historical project of liberation for the crisis at the US-Mexico border.

Theological and Socio-Analytical Methodology

As Clodovis Boff (2005, 30) once advised, theology must first of all incline its ear to the social sciences if it hopes to be liberating, while also avoiding the collapse of one distinct discipline into another. As such, for political theology, the social sciences will be genuinely constitutive of what theology can say and what can be its theoretical organization

(Boff 2005, 30). And as with any contextual theology, its historical situation and its particular theological concerns will also be mutually constitutive of each other. Political theology in general and liberation theology in particular function to sensitize people of faith to what is believed to be God's will in a specific historical setting and to inspire their commitment to participating in God's mission of reconciliation in that setting. Thus the aim in political theology is to bring faith and action together more effectively (Sousa Santos 2009).

First, Liberation theology is distinct not only for its content but also for its method. Undergirding this method is the Judeo-Christian-theological commitment to the preferential option for the poor and the oppressed and to seeing change realized for the people in these circumstances. Second, there is the process of sociohistorical analysis and the examination of the structures in place that enable subjugation. Finally, there is the critical-theological reflection on praxis for carrying out action that contributes to the goal of liberation in light of the unjust conditions in place. Hence, liberation theology is praxis in history and society—that is, critical reflection on action already enacted and largely informed by the context and concerns of a given situation (Metz 1980, 73). As such, it begins by way of sociohistorical analysis.

The Larger Context: Globalization

The crisis in Mexico caused by the drug trade is seen here to be exemplary of the more universal context of globalization itself. Globalization is understood in this case as a process or set of processes that embodies a transformation in the spatial organization of social relations and transactions in terms of increased intensity, extensity, velocity and impact (Held et al. 1999, 16). These relations and transactions are not only economic and political in nature but also cultural and environmental.

They involve changing and complex regimes of differentiation and homogenization that have constructed new paths and limits for global economic flows. Other common byproducts include the rapid reconfiguration of territories especially with respect to patterns of economic exchange. The invisibility of economic power structures and their ability to develop independently of legitimate political power is a key challenge brought about by globalization. This challenge is exacerbated by the permeation and extension of this economic power beyond national borders.

Moreover, the process of globalization is replete with contradictions, uncertainties, and unevenness. For this reason, globalization is not simply coterminous with neoliberalism.[2] In other words, few globalizing factors at work are purely economic and therefore cannot be reduced to the logic of free trade and the international division of labor or class.

At the same time, globalization can still be conceived in many respects as a context in which "devising alternatives to neoliberal market capitalism has become increasingly difficult" (Alcoff and Sáenz 2003, 200). International deregulation through trade agreements is one of the chief ways the empire of global capitalism is expanded. In the case of the US-Mexico border, NAFTA brought about increases in foreign direct investment, but the tradeoff has been a less developed and more dependent Mexican economy in many respects. Mexico has been forced to move away from an agriculturally dominant society to an economy represented by manufacturing, commerce, and services (Camp 2007, 247). The overall impact has varied tremendously depending on the region.

With regard to drug trafficking, just as production has been outsourced in the age of globalization, so too have many aspects of organized violence. States have a monopoly on the ability to legitimize violence but cannot monopolize violence itself. With the extraordinary coercive power of illicit cartel networks, the drug war is one example of this kind of violence.

The Mexico Drug War Itself

The major impetus for unrest in the border region depends on the demand for drugs in metropolitan centers in the United States and the supply from Colombia. Once a kilo of cocaine reaches the streets in the United States, it will be worth $100,000, or about $100 a gram. In the Colombian countryside the same substance is worth $3,000, or about three dollars a gram. The single greatest contributor to this giant surplus value is believed to be the illegality and therefore added political risk of the production, transportation, and consumption of the drugs themselves. Investigative journalist John Gibler explains that

> illegality also requires that one [bolster] the moral discourse of prohibition with massive infusion of funds into armies and law-enforcement agencies. These infusions in turn require the production of arrests and drug seizures. Competitors in the drug economy use this need as a way to eliminate opponents and rivals, tipping off federal authorities to the whereabouts of [enemy stashes and hideouts]. (2011, 35)

In this context, illegality adds another more blatant complication: every dispute within the industry must be settled outside the law. Rather than merely engaging in a competitive price war, the most common method of conflict resolution in an illegal business culture rampant with cash is contract murder (Gibler 2011, 38).

As of 2011, the polls taken by the Transborder Institute at the University of San Diego estimate that approximately 50,000 Mexicans have died since 2006 as a result of the conflict and as a result of the competition at the border for trade smuggling routes between the different DTOs (drug trafficking organizations) to secure their gain from the multibillion dollars' worth of narcotics that cross the border every year (2011). Significantly more killings have happened in the border city of Juarez than anywhere else. Less than 5 percent of these cases have been or are ever likely to be investigated. Moreover, many of the murders are spectacular, stylized, and torturous in nature. For this reason, it is not uncommon for the violence of the drug war to be called "narcoterrorism"—though this kind of terrorism differs markedly from others in that it seems to be primarily motivated by competition for control of revenue in the industry.

Most critics of the drug war believe that the drug trade and the present laws against drug trafficking are mutually reinforcing. Gibler argues that

> the blood and chaos that accompany drug trafficking from Mexico into the United States are inextricably related to the simultaneous demand within the U.S. population for the [drugs], and the insistence of U.S. politicians on an ideological commitment to prohibition that seeks to veil prohibition's use for social control. (2011, 43)

In response, though US policy has not stopped the flow of drugs, it has managed to outsource most of the killing (Gibler 2011, 203). With dozens of reporters in Mexico gunned down or disappeared since 2008, the DTOs are especially skilled at silencing those who speak out. The targets seem to be anyone with access to major media channels, or anybody who annunciates facts that could be bad for business (Gibler 2011, 23).

Narcoterrorism is essentially an effort to coerce the media and scare others away from cooperating with law enforcement. Furthermore, it is estimated by Mexico's own government that the DTOs have infiltrated as much as half of the municipal police force. At the same time, "producing arrests is a necessary feature of the industry, and so, like murder, arrest becomes a way of settling accounts or invading territory" (Gibler 2011, 23). Thus, the culpable and the innocent are confused, and the hybridity of the drug war zone is highlighted.

The temptation on the part of US citizens is often to dismiss organized crime as outside the "clean legal system," rather than to recognize how interwoven official government is in drug trafficking on *both* sides of the border. This is what makes the US government's deployment of the phrase "war on drugs" so misleading. It is well known by even some DEA officials that the drug war machinery suffers from an industrial complex that to some extent causes the very disease it aims to cure, but this is a powerful sector of government that employs thousands of people and can easily lobby for itself (Campbell 2009, 10).

For Mexico's antidrug campaign, however, which was amplified by President Felipe Calderon in 2006, the most important audience is the United States—both its media and political representatives. It has even been argued that, despite what looks like an intense turf battle on the surface, politicians at the national level in Mexico might have good reason not to substantially disrupt DTO operations for the risk of having their past collusions exposed before an election (Stratfor Global Intelligence 2012).

So at one level, victims sometimes become victimizers. Those immediately impacted by declining employment opportunities, for instance, can end up on the Sinaloa or Zeta cartel payroll. This makes them servants to the system in which their fate is often sealed, as many low-paid traffickers and snitches are brutally executed after being intercepted by rival gangs. Videos of these executions circulate on the internet to incite fear, and bodies are left on public display.

Meanwhile, however, those uninvolved in trafficking are commonly caught in the crossfire. At another level then, some binaries remain, and it may be possible to make a few general distinctions between the oppressors and those being oppressed. It seems clear that free trade zoning coupled with continued illegalization—all of which is encouraged or permitted by a corrupt legal system in parts of Mexico—has largely contributed to the creation of a deregulated capitalist "laboratory," which, in the words of author Charles Bowden, has become "the global economy's new killing field" (Bowden 2010). The oppressor then, appears to be a structural economic and legal framework that is bolstered by consumers, misinformed or self-seeking political stakeholders, and ruthless DTO leadership.

Conversely, the oppressed are the low-wage dealers and transporters, the addicts without treatment, the overly incarcerated minorities in the United States, the displaced Mexican migrants, and the thousands who have been abused or killed mostly due to a lack of lawfulness in general (poor teenage women and their activist mothers, among others).

Furthermore, this list notes that the two groups are not simply separated by their citizenship. The border is significant but by no means an all-determining factor. In sum, the weight of these asymmetrical relationships falls heaviest on the socially and materially impoverished, which makes a liberationist theological consideration especially appropriate.

A Brief Theological Reflection

From a Christian political-theological perspective, there are two tasks. First, there is a response to the cry for liberation from the current oppressive situation in view of a preferential option for the poor and the victimized. Christians of conscience and conviction about the need for solidarity of Mexicans and Americans will be led to heed the demands placed on them by the voices of these persons being erased from history and those of their orphans and widows left behind. Second, one can speak about the solidarity that Christians profess God to have with the suffering victims of this crisis through the person of Jesus Christ.

Jesus is known through the hermeneutic of liberation in living, dying, and being resurrected as God incarnate who embodies solidarity with those whose lives have been disappeared in this battle (Sobrino 1994, 315). By announcing both judgment of unjust power and freedom for captives, the poor and the marginalized, Jesus stands firmly within the Jewish prophetic tradition as one who was shunned for criticizing the political and religious status quo. In his death, Christ's blood exposes and protests the violence and injustice of the drug lords and all other complicit actors, reflects the sin and wickedness of their deeds, and yet also declares forgiveness and justification to the penitent (Park 2009, 74). Jesus cried out from the cross against the torture, murder, exploitation, and injustice of the Mexican drug war, just as he denounced the rest of history's atrocities (Park 2009, 75).

In his life, Jesus proclaimed the *basilea theou*, or reign of God, which might be more appropriately termed "God's economy" or the "divine commonwealth." In this economy, power is not granted *de facto* to the materially powerful, but rather to the one whose way is anchored in justice for everyone. The hegemony and ordering of the drug trade economy is abolished by this alternative vision—a vision that refuses to ignore the plight of the oppressed in the pursuit of its goal and regards no human being as less than a fellow subject.

Jesus's crucifixion is yet another symbol of God's solidarity with the victim of the drug war. In one sense, it can be treated simply as a prophet's fate. Jesus's death came as a consequence of the kind of life he led and because of what he said and did. He got in the way of political and religious leaders with imperial agendas. Many other human beings have been "crucified," and they too are called sons and daughters of God by Jesus. By participating in human nature and suffering like so many others have, Jesus demonstrates something about what God is like. God in Jesus's humanity is a fellow-sufferer. Through Jesus, God understands the plight of the victimized.

More specifically, the manner in which Jesus died is astonishingly analogous to the execution practices of the drug cartels. "Criminals" were crucified at the time not so much for what they did, but for the degree to which they were perceived as a threat to Roman security and sovereignty (Crossan 2007, 137). Jesus was replacing Barabbas, the insurrectionist. The crucifixion was meant to be a public and fear-inciting inscription of Roman territory on anti-imperial bodies. The drug cartels are similarly interested in intimidation and leaving their signage on victims' mutilated corpses. "This is what happens to all those who oppose us," they warn.

Third, by confessing the resurrection, God's mission in Christ is not only one of compassion and solidarity but also of salvation. Here the nature of God's power is contrasted with that of the empire, exerted conversely in a just and righteous fashion. Moreover, this power is not reducible to the political realm alone. Rather, it is ontological and vital, and it mysteriously raises Jesus from the grave, as the scriptures and the creeds of orthodoxy testify. For the victims of the world throughout history in general and of drug-related violence in Mexico in particular, some recourse to hope can be found in this promise.

In his life, Jesus broke down social barriers and included the outcast—those like the drug dealer, the prisoner, the addict, and the victimized woman. Jesus's suffering and death makes it clear that the victims of violence are not all dying because of their guilt or uncleanness (Park 2004, 75)—unlike much of what the popular media and the Mexican government would lead the public to believe. Jesus's willingness to lay down his life is inspiration to all of the families and friends of dead journalists and reminds that their sacrifices have not been in vain. Finally, the resurrection eases the fear of mortality, giving survivors the courage to resist and make sacrifices while also instilling the hope that death might not get the final word.

Of course this represents just one type of theological response in what is otherwise now more broadly called an interreligious stream of liberationist thought, so others must also be urged to give their own interpretation. The point is that these Mexican brothers and sisters are the suffering neighbors of US citizens, and in the words of economist Ha-Joon Chang (2008), we have been bad Samaritans. Nevertheless, blaming the right group is less important than recognizing the justification and need for solidarity from one's particular vantage point—and responding by living with greater economic responsibility.

Ethical Response

Upon preliminary observation, it seems that any kind of liberating political action will probably require breaking the taboo on debate and reform of drug and free trade policy. Utopian visions are of little use in this predicament, and a theological criticism must eventually be grounded in practical terms lest it function to reinscribe the domination of political indifference. Juarez did not become possibly the most violent and deadly city in the world overnight. Nor is its current condition accidental. Despite many other enabling factors, the crisis appears to be most basically a result of the sheer power of unregulated market forces and its ability to bring out the worst in people—driving some to value recreational psychoactive stimulus, the securitization of cash flow, or the appearance of civility over human life itself.

As anthropologist and sociologist of the drug war Howard Campbell summarizes, "The consuming countries clearly have the most power in this context—power to cut domestic drug demand, the power to pressure the policies of drug-producing countries and otherwise meddle in their internal affairs, the power to demonize and otherwise stigmatize producers" (2009, 10). From a liberationist standpoint, the social and structural sins of the conflict should be named, which, in addition to denouncing the cruelty itself, should entail a *new* stigmatization of casual drug use and of failure to open the floor for dialogue about different regulatory strategies at the mainstream political level. Right now in most of the country, and in most instances, to consume these substances illegally is to at least indirectly participate in fueling the bloodshed. What should be instilled in the minds of American consumers, therefore, is a self-critical ethic that uncovers the illusion of personal, private sin associated with social use of narcotics and conversely underscores the urgency of the collective harm done by funding this ruthlessly profit-seeking industry. Change in US policy toward narcotics and trade might lead to the reduction of rampant murder, the impunity of entire regions, mass incarceration, disguised repression, excessive spending to fight the war, and the pretext for US interference in drug-producing countries. This is reason enough for the discussion to be welcomed and for experimentation with new policies to be encouraged, because whatever the most just and liberating solution is, the policies currently in effect are not achieving it.

There are many things that Mexicans and the Mexican government can and should consider doing. Responsibility for this crisis falls on both parties, and obviously the United States and its population is in no place to unilaterally advise the Mexican people. Nonetheless, given the preceding assessment, the most pressing and potentially liberating steps to be taken are likely only possible from the northern side of the border. For the United States to initiate this sort of neighborly action would be a revolutionary measure in the direction of solidarity with Mexico and international economic responsibility.

Notes

1. What is presented here does not exhibit a rigorous empirical study of all the best data available, and this would certainly need to be part of the larger project. The purpose then is not to make detailed recommendations for policy change so much as to raise awareness, introduce the topic, and broadly explicate the key structural features and likely causes of the conflict so as to signal toward possible paths forward. In doing so, however, certain suggestions regarding which political issues are most pertinent will nonetheless be clearly insinuated.

2. Neoliberalism is understood here as the dominant Western economic ideology that is characterized by trust in self-interest–driven free market competition with very limited government interference as the best strategy both domestically *and* internationally for bringing about the greatest good for the greatest number of people in the long run.

Bibliography

Alcoff, L. N., and M. Sáenz. 2003. *Latin American Perspectives on Globalization: Ethics, Politics, and Alternative Visions*. Lanham: Rowman & Littlefield.

Boff, C. 2005. *Theology and Praxis: Epistemological Foundations*. Eugene: Wipf & Stock.

Bowden, C. 2010. *Murder City: Ciudad Juarez and the Global Economy's New Killing Fields*. Asbury Park: Nation Books.

Camp, R. 2007. *Politics in Mexico: The Democratic Consoludation*. New York: Oxford University Press.

Campbell, H. 2009. *Drug War Zone: Frontline Dispatches from the Streets of El Paso and Juárez*. Austin: University of Texas Press.

Chang, H. J. 2008. *Bad Samaritans: The Myth of Free Trade and the Secret History of Capitalism.* New York: Bloomsbury.

Crossan, J. D. 2007. *God and Empire: Jesus against Rome, Then and Now.* New York: HarperOne.

Gibler, J. 2011. *To Die in Mexico: Dispatches from Inside the Drug War.* San Francisco: City Lights.

Held, D., Anthony McGrew, David Goldblatt, and Jonathan Perraton. 1999. *Global Transformations: Politics, Economics and Culture.* Stanford: Stanford University Press.

Metz, J. B. 1980. *Faith in History and Society: Toward a Practical Fundamental Theology.* New York: Seabury.

Park, A. 2004. *From Hurt to Healing: A Theology of the Wounded.* Nashville: Abingdon.

———. 2009. *Triune Atonement: Christ's Healing for Sinners, Victims, and the Whole Creation.* Louisville: Westminster John Knox.

Sobrino, J. 1994. *Jesus the Liberator: A Historical Theological Reading of Jesus of Nazareth.* Maryknoll: Orbis Books.

Sousa Santos, B. 2009. "If God were a Human Rights Activist: Human Rights and the Challenge of Political Theologies." *Law Social Justice and Global Development.* Festschrift for Upendra Baxi.

Stratfor Global Intelligence. 2012. "Mexico's Presidential Election and Cartel War." http://www.stratfor.com/weekly/mexicos-presidential-election-and-cartel-war/. Accessed February 16, 2012.

University of San Diego Transborder Institute. Drug Violence Report for 2011. http://justiceinmexico.org/resources-2/drug-violence/. Accessed December 13, 2011.

CHAPTER 19

Doing Liberation Theology as a Resistive Performance

Malik J. Sales
mjsales.ckr@gmail.com

Learn from the past and work for the future/...And the future of the
world is in your hands/
— Glover, Griffin, and Robinson, 1984

I was five years old when I first heard that rhyme by Melle Mel. The
song, "Beat Street Breakdown," arrested and still arrests my attention. When I hear the song, it is like Melle Mel is right in front of
me and forcing me into a crisis. Will I pay attention to him or will I turn
my head and ignore his cry? The song is confrontational, loud, bold,
searing, and heartfelt. I could not understand everything he said, but
the *way* he spit that verse—the way he delivered his lines made me take
pause. When I got older and analyzed the content of the lyrics, non-
inclusive language notwithstanding, I realized the historical analysis,
hope, and prophetic compassion behind Melle Mel's wordplay. I realized
how performance was a part of any movement for liberation. The struggle to resist injurious, death-dealing, and meaning-defeating events and
sagas—this struggle feeds off the quest for life-giving possibilities and
often times uses whatever means it can to instantiate itself. Resistance
is a dynamic process, which includes economics, politics, religion, communities, aesthetics, etcetera, even music and sometimes hip-hop. A
struggle for resistance comes with a soundtrack. And although we could
never quantify them or claim that they are the inexhaustible key to
transformation, performances—in this case, musical expression—continue to help us imagine and work toward justice, mercy, and peace in

an ambivalent world. However, it was not just Melle Mel's words that grabbed my attention but the ways the words are *performed*, the accompaniment of instruments and synthesizers, and the thought-provoking images that spawned from his verse. My academic side forgets this from time to time, but concepts, projects, and theories have attitude and emotion behind them. In the words of Augusto Boal, the aesthetic communication of sound, images, words, and particularly theater possess the ability to transform us into "spect-actors."[1] For Boal, art has strong practical implications for rethinking the various avenues to approach liberation. He writes, "'Spectator' is a bad word! The spectator is less than a man [sic] and it is necessary to humanize him, to restore him his capacity of action in all its fullness. He too must be a subject, an actor on an equal plane as those generally accepted as actors, who must also be spectators" (Boal 1985, 155).

And while performance has practical implications, it also possesses epistemological power as well. For instance, "Beat Street Breakdown" reminds us of the multiplicity of oppression and suffering from a moral sense, but the causes of suffering do not stay there. The problems this world faces are beyond human wrongdoing, even though human wrongdoing is exceptionally flagrant. Or as Curtis Mayfield (1997) said in the funk classic "Freddie's Dead," "We're all built up with progress, but sometimes I must confess, We can deal with rockets and dreams, but reality what does it mean? Ain't nothing said, cuz Freddie's dead." Mayfield, with his soulful, incisive singing, underscores the limits of anthropocentrism and progressivism within even the best of our intentions, ingenuity, and theology. Some things in reality do not depend on human cooperation, knowledge, or permission in order to exist, yet they influence us just the same, particularly those who are oppressed—those who are most vulnerable to not only structural power but also disease and famine. What these few examples hope to highlight is this: epistemologically, performance has a way of incorporating the various and the multiple, and practically, performance has the ability to simultaneously stimulate our feeling, thinking, and acting.[2] Now what do such observations have to do with liberation theology?

In *The Future of Liberation Theology*, Ivan Petrella (2006, vii) cogently argues that today, liberation theologies have *primarily* become academic reflection disassociated from what he calls "historical projects," that is "models of political and economic organization that would replace an unjust status quo." In Petrella's assessment, historical projects give content to theological reflection, and without such projects, concepts central to liberation theology (Latin American in this instance) such as "the preferential option for the poor," "liberation," and the "Reign of God" become empty and easily coopted by those in power.[3]

Although I agree that historical projects must be constructed, I do not think that such a reinvigoration must *only* be in the realm of economics and politics. However, this must be made clear: we *desperately* need political and economic historical projects of resistance and liberation. Without these two dimensions, any real attempt to historically transform the deleterious and death-dealing conditions of our planet, ecosystem, and human relationships is altogether naïve, suspect, and bankrupt. However, I believe these two dimensions are not enough. It is not altogether apparent that liberationist methodology can *only* be effective in the area of collective, systemic human wrongdoing. Such a claim, I believe sells liberation and transformational theologies short, due to the fact that they are theologies that attempt to be in tune with *those who suffer disproportionately*, which includes but is not exhausted by politics and economics. Yes, Gustavo Gutiérrez wrote that a theology of liberation was constituted as "critical reflection on historical praxis" (1988, 5), but the Peruvian theologian also wrote these words: "Human suffering, involvement with it, and the questions it raises about God are in fact one point of departure and one central theme in the theology of liberation" (1985, xv). Contextual theologies of transformation, in all their varieties, are fundamentally, inextricably, and self-consciously linked to the historicity of suffering and evil, albeit collective suffering and evil.

Therefore, liberation theologies can also be seen as contemporary soteriologies that take seriously the concrete and visceral questions asked when traversing the various undersides of history. And certain undersides are not only caused by human wrongdoing but also by rubble and flooding in the wake of natural disasters, such as earthquakes in Haiti and Hurricane Katrina. Here, I recall the insight of Karen Baker-Fletcher, namely that African-American performative art forms (spirituals, the blues, jazz, and hip-hop) provide intelligible ways of grasping and responding to injury, death, and meaninglessness.[4] In light of such a realization, I contend that historical projects of resistance should *attempt* to respond to and consider disproportionate suffering, damage, and death in a *myriad of ways* and *no matter the causes*. Stated bluntly, we need all the responses, alternatives, and analyses we can get in the long run and in the meantime.

All concepts and projects of resistance/liberation are *ambivalent* in its relationship to damaging, death-dealing, and despairing conditions. Unfortunately, any concept/act can be used to support oppressive systems or to obscure disproportionate suffering, even a verse from Melle Mel. This is why we must continuously produce variegated compassionate, prophetic, and hope-filled projects. Singular forms of analyses and projects, even when helpful and resistive, are easily co-opted. Co-optation, thus understood, is not just "taking up" or "assimilation"; in the final analysis, it is a matter of neutralization. And what has been neutralized is, in the end, *possibilities*.

Performance theory, though not exhaustive, provides a hybrid space that allows me to construct/analyze historical projects, while simultaneously granting me a phenomenological space to theorize about the world in which we live, including the substantial role of non-human activity. My primary interlocutor in this discipline is the performance theorist, Erika Fischer-Lichte. For Fischer-Lichte, performance is not primarily a work of art, independent of its creator and subject to the infinite interpretations of spectators. Rather, performance is an "interactive" and "confrontational" *event* that destabilizes and sometimes collapses the boundaries between "subject and object" and "signified and signifier," which can realign "the interconnection between feeling, thinking, acting." In short, we do not just interpret a performance; we *experience* it corporeally. We oscillate between the roles of actor and spectator; we are confronted with the reality of the event even as and sometimes before we interpret it, and through this ambivalent and unpredictable experience, a moment of transformation becomes *possible* (Fischer-Lichte 2008, 16–18, 22–25). Realigning the ways we feel, think, and act stimulates this possibility.

This transformative understanding of performance is embodied in the word "resistance," which can take on many shapes in its confrontation with damaging and destructive forces. Resistance means being affected by, identifying, subverting, surviving, and/or transforming injury, death, and meaninglessness. In other words, resistive performance is multifaceted, carrying both epistemological and active dimensions, and it is diverse in its confrontations with deleterious conditions that bring about dehumanization, suffering, and hopelessness, but rarely if ever, does one project run the gamut from affectation to transformation. As I draw this essay to a close let me briefly highlight the two major reasons I have chosen to use this academic discipline and Fischer-Lichte in particular.

First, Fischer-Lichte inherently assumes that *multiple factors* make up any performance. And performance here is understood as an *unrepeatable event*. By way of analogy, Fischer-Lichte's performance theory provides a substantial basis for the construction of a theological epistemology of injury, death, and meaninglessness. In the same way Fischer-Lichte views performance as an interactive and confrontational event that *happens* at a particular place and time; I contend that the same can be said of what has traditionally been called "evil." My use of the phrase "injury, death, and meaninglessness" is a sober attempt to highlight the multiplicity of suffering, which is caused at times by multiple factors, including but not limited to structural sin. In addition, Fischer-Lichte is repeatedly clear on this one point: because performance is an event that happens due to the bodily co-presence of actors, spectators, and staging at a particular juncture in space/time, it cannot be repeated or completely predetermined. In the case of a stage play, for instance, the performance *as event* is not only limited to the actors or script but also to the lighting, the audience, the *time and space of its happening/reception*, and more.

In other words, multiplicity and interdependence is a *given*. It is such compositional variance in space-time that makes any event, not just a performance, unrepeatable and unique. Following Max Hermann, Fischer-Lichte maintains that "this dynamic and wholly unpredictable process *precludes the expression and transmission of predetermined meanings*; the performance itself generates its meanings" (2008, 35; italics mine). Performance theory takes for granted the compositionality not only of performance but also of the world we inhabit. Such a perspective would be indispensable to a theology that seeks to move beyond human sin and uncover the concomitant factors that cause events and sagas of injury, death, and meaninglessness, with a keen eye on those who are oppressed. For instance, addressing concrete problems such as African Americans' greater risk for diabetes,[5] heart disease,[6] and high blood pressure[7] requires one to consider not only socioeconomic factors but also genetic predisposition, choice of diet, and so on. Likewise, performance theory proves extremely helpful in creating and appreciating multiple responses to woeful events in order to move beyond a single, typifying salvific event.

My final point: performance theory allows liberation theology to see itself as a *performative event*. By highlighting the performative dimension of liberation theology, I intend to move it beyond "discourse" or "theory" (which is traditionally set over against practice) toward a potential historical project of resistance. The performative dimension of theology grants any theological project the ability to inform and change the epistemology, praxis, and concerns of a person and/or group. As an academic discourse, liberation theology, in varying degrees, has transformative power, but academic prose is not the only way liberation theology "performs" itself. Indeed, there are other mediums, such as musical performance. Fundamentally, doing liberation theology as a resistive performance is an attempt to call attention and respond to injurious, death-dealing, and meaning-defeating moments and sagas through the use of multiple forms of communication. It is a theology that shouts with Melle Mel, who says, "Search for justice and what do you find, you find just us in the unemployment line, you find just us sweating from dawn to dusk, there's no justice, it's just us." This is a theology that underscores the many soundtracks and scores that lament life and death, yet still cry out for liberation and deliverance. This is doing liberation theology as a resistive performance.

Notes

1. "Spect-actors are invited to come on stage and reveal by means of theatre – rather than just by using words – the thoughts, desires and strategies that can suggest, to the group to which they belong, a palette of possible alternatives of their own invention. This theatre should be a rehearsal for action in real life rather than an end in itself" (Boal 2006, 13, 6).
2. Augusto Boal holds that one of the primary characteristics of "aesthetic communication" is its ability to transcend the limiting capacities of "words and sets." He writes, "Words are the work and the instrument of reason: we have to transcend them and look for forms of communication which are not just rational, but also sensory—aesthetic communications." The work of an artist therefore is to perceive and reveal the unicities "hidden by the simplification of the language which names them and senses which group them without perceiving them" (Boal 2006, 16–17).
3. Petrella writes, "The way these elements are defended [by theologians such as Gustavo Gutiérrez], however, exacts too high a cost. What allows this position to work is the emptying of the idea defended. It is no longer clear what the preferential option for the poor, the Reign of God, and liberation mean in practice without some sort of social scientific mediation, whether Marxist or not; without such mediation it remains impossible to provide alternatives to the current global order" (2006, 4).
4. "Where suffering, evil, hatred, unnecessary violence, and injustice exist, the entire earth 'cries out' to God… Those who lament evil are not irrational. They are imbued with reason. This reason is integrated with *feeling*, which is the experience of reality. Such is the intelligence of the spirituals, blues, jazz, and hip-hop" (Baker-Fletcher 2006, 15).
5. "African Americans are twice as likely to be diagnosed with diabetes as non-Hispanic whites. In addition, they are more likely to suffer complications from diabetes, such as end-stage renal disease and lower extremity amputations. Although African Americans have the same or lower rate of high

cholesterol as their non-Hispanic white counterparts, they are more likely to have high blood pressure." Health and Humans Services Office of Minority Health, "Diabetes and African Americans," http://minorityhealth.hhs.gov /templates/content.aspx?ID=3017 (accessed January 14, 2011).

6. "African American adults are more likely to be diagnosed with coronary heart disease, and they are more likely to die from heart disease. Although African American adults are 40 percent more likely to have high blood pressure, they are 10 percent less likely than their non-Hispanic White counterparts to have their blood pressure under control." Health and Human Services Office of Minority Health, "Heart Disease and African Americans," http://minorityhealth.hhs.gov/templates/content .aspx?ID=3018 (accessed January 14, 2011).

7. "African Americans develop high blood pressure more often, and at an earlier age, than whites and Mexican Americans do. Among African Americans, more women than men have the condition." Centers for Disease Control, "High Blood Pressure Facts," http://www.cdc.gov/bloodpressure /facts.htm (accessed January 14, 2011).

Bibliography

Baker-Fletcher, K. 2006. *Dancing with God: The Trinity from a Womanist Perspective.* St. Louis: Chalice.

Boal, A. 1985. *Theatre of the Oppressed.* Translated by A. Charles and Maria-Odilia Leal McBride. New York: Theatre Communications Group.

———. 2006. *Aesthetics of the Oppressed.* Translated by Adrian Jackson. New York: Routledge.

Fischer-Lichte, E. 2008. *The Transformative Power of Performance: A New Aesthetics.* Translated by Saskya Iris Jain. New York: Routledge.

Glover, M., R. Griffin, and S. Robinson. 1984. "Beat Street Breakdown." In *Beat Street Soundtrack* (Original Soundtrack), performed by Melle Mel, Atlantic Records 80154, Cassette Tape.

Gutiérrez, G. 1985. *On Job: God Talk and the Suffering of the Innocent.* Translated by Matthew J. O'Connell. Maryknoll: Orbis Books.

———. 1988. *A Theology of Liberation: History, Politics, and Salvation.* Translated and edited by Sister Caridad Inda and John Eagleson. Maryknoll: Orbis Books.

Mayfield, C. 1997. "Freddie's Dead." In *The Ultimate Curtis Mayfield*, Recall (UK) SMDCD 105, Compact Disc.

Petrella, I. 2006. *The Future of Liberation Theology: An Argument and Manifesto*, London: SCM.

Conclusion

Thia Cooper
tcooper@gac.edu

Where do we go from here? These 19 chapters show the breadth and depth of liberation theologies and share many overlapping themes. Theology emerges from practice. Liberation theologies act. Talking without acting does not liberate. Liberationists act in many realms and continue to recognize new realms in which oppression exists.

Liberation theologies have matured since their beginnings of fighting economic and political repression. We see that the field encompasses aspects as diverse as empire, nature, class, capitalism, genocide, political repression, violence, marginalization, religious oppression, race, migration, feminism, human rights, revolution, community, theological education, education in general, the arts, the drug trade, indigeneity, sex, sexuality, gender, just to name a few. Theologies of liberation point out the elephant in the room. They continue to shed light on contexts ignored by those with power.

Liberationists continue resisting oppression, countering hegemony, examining structures of oppression. These include some of the oppression we participate in over others, even as we ourselves might be oppressed. We have myriad ways of exercising our own power to harm others personally and institutionally. Walz notes this in arguing that gender theology must be intercultural, not defined or dominated by a Euro-American concept of gender. Countering oppression must be accompanied by a search for alternatives in order not to replicate oppressive behavior.

Liberation theologies are on the side of the poor and marginalized, whether that marginalization be due to economics, politics, ecology, race, ethnicity, colonization, religion, gender, sexuality, or others. This includes the fact that human beings themselves must be prioritized over economic or political concepts, and the community above the individual. I appreciate Ruether's contribution reminding us that those of us who are powerful must give up our power. It may be that individually some give up wealth to join the poor but this needs to happen structurally too, with businesses and nation-states. This is true of liberation theology itself. Liberation practices do not require a PhD or that one be part of the academy. In the academy we tend to prioritize those more established in the field, which I think may be to our peril. We definitely prioritize a dead white male history. And we have acrobatically whitewashed people out, as Townes notes.

For me, as a white woman living and working in the United States, it is not as simple as letting go of power individually. I have that aspect to contend with and the aspects in which I am oppressed, for example, my gender. I am also part of a web of institutions, which oppress or can be oppressed. This is a fruitful area on which to focus in the future, as the importance of intersections is increasingly recognized.

Several of the authors note that we need to deeply understand specific contexts *and* help each other to work together. Liberation theologies take context seriously and work to find shared contexts because no one context can be prioritized alone. Valentin's notion of bringing together socioeconomic and cultural injustices to work together for recognition and redistribution is an important one that you see in several of the essays including Rieger's. Sinclair's work put this into practice with Cone and Marx. No context is extraneous. Working together to overthrow hegemony and create spaces of resistance is more effective than competing amongst ourselves. And yet current structures, current elites, attempt to leave only a small space for "context," in which they want us to compete. In contrast, we need to build a coalition to overturn traditional theology and move forward the course of liberation.

There is, I think, room for much more theological creativity as Valentin points out. Theological thoughts to be taken forward could include: God sees that creation is good; humans are to steward it. Love God and love one's neighbor as oneself. God is a victim with the victims. Jesus has been crucified once again, with each victim: victims of the class system, victims of political repression such as Palestinians, victims of the drug trade, and so forth. There is also Paul's notion of us as a body where if one part suffers, all parts suffer with it. And finally, in the search for alternatives, the earliest Christian communities in Acts can help. While this search for alternatives used to be talked about in terms of a new heaven and a new earth, this is not articulated by any of our authors here. This and other themes have shifted over time. I hope the reading of this book has sparked additional theological themes for you to take forward, whatever your faith tradition.

Liberation theologies look for liberating practices in communities, listen to new voices, and articulate what is seen and heard. This is a theology "of" the people, not for the people, the embodied theology of which Marcos speaks. While creative theologies are needed, they need to emerge from practice and be put back into practice in historical projects as Petrella notes. This theological creativity should come from a variety of religious traditions, not simply Christianity because it runs the risk of hegemony, as it has in other situations, as Marcos, Raheb, and Tinker point out in particular. Jewish, Muslim, and other liberation theologies, some linked to the Arab Spring, appear to be emerging. We are also seeing connections with the Occupy Movement. Perhaps this could also lead to liberationists being trained in and to speak about fields outside theology.

In particular, liberation theologies need to focus on youth. Raheb notes the importance of youth in his article on Arab Revolutions, and I think it echoes in other realms too. There are three influential areas in our society today that remain under-analyzed: sport, music, and film. The PhD students are beginning to analyze some of this. Youth are also the majority of migrants, as Medina notes in the Canadian context and the drug trade tends to have the young as its victims, and as the sellers and users of drugs. There are many further issues that could be addressed with regard to youth and beyond: the prison system, the armed forces, war, generalized violence, access to water and food, and so on.

As I try to teach liberation theologies, it is tempting to try to streamline and "sanitize" them, to enable students to choose one strand. However, I realize this tendency will not lead to future liberations; it will only enable another hegemony, similar to what Te Paa faced in her theological education. The academy can counter this though and nurture practices and habits of thought that can encourage further liberation practices.

Rather than putting our energies into ignoring the elephants in the room, I'd like for us to acknowledge them, talk about them, welcome them. So let me leave you with one question. What is the elephant in the room for you that no one seems to speak about?

Further Suggested Readings

Althaus-Reid, M., ed. 2006. *Liberation Theology and Sexuality*. London: Ashgate.

Cannon, K. G., E. M. Townes, and A. D. Sims, eds. 2001. *Womanist Theological Ethics: A Reader*. Louisville: Westminster John Knox.

Copeland, M. S. 2009. *Enfleshing Freedom: Body, Race, and Being*. Minneapolis: Fortress.

Diop, B. B. 2006. *Murambi, the Book of Bones: A Novel*. Bloomington and Indianapolis: Indiana University Press.

Dussel. E. 2013. *Ethics of Liberation in the Age of Globalization and Exclusion*. Durham: Duke University Press.

Espin, O. 2007. *Grace and Humanness*. Maryknoll: Orbis Books.

Keller, C., M. Rivera, and M. Nausner, eds. 2004. *Postcolonial Theologies: Divinity and Empire*. St. Louis: Chalice.

Lewis, H. 2007. *Deaf Liberation Theology*. London: Ashgate.

Longchar, W. 2012. "Indigenous Theology in Asia: Issues and Perspectives." In *Asian Theology on the Way: Christianity, Culture and Context*, ed. P. Jesudason and R. Rajkumar, 83–96. London: SPCK.

Mann, B. 2000. *Iroquoian Women: The Gantowisas*. New York: Peter Lang.

Marcos, S. 2010. *Women in Indigenous Religions*. Santa Barbara: Praeger.

McKibben, B. 2010. *Eaarth: Making Life on a Tough New Planet*. New York: Times Books.

Míguez, N., J. Rieger, and J. M. Sung. 2009. *Beyond the Spirit of Empire*. London: SCM.

Morris, G. 2003. "Vine Deloria, Jr. and the Development of a Contemporary Critique of Indigenous Peoples and International Relations." In *Native Voices: American Indian Identity and Resistance*, ed. R. A. Grounds, G. E. Tinker, and D. E. Wilkins, 97–154. Lawrence: University of Kansas Press.

Nanko-Fernandez, C. 2010. *Theologizing en Espanglish: Context, Community and Ministry*. Maryknoll: Orbis Books.

Petrella, I. 2008. *Beyond Liberation Theology: A Polemic*. London: SCM.

Raheb, M. ed. 2012. *The Biblical Text in the Context of Occupation: Towards a New Hermeneutics of Liberation*. Bethlehem: Diyar.

Regan, E. 2010. *Theology and the Boundary Discourse of Human Rights*, Washington, DC: Georgetown University Press.

Rieger, J., and Kwok, P. 2012. *Occupy Religion: Theology of the Multitude*. Lanham: Rowman and Littlefield.

Rowland, C., ed. 2007. *The Cambridge Companion to Liberation Theology*. Cambridge: Cambridge University Press.

Ruether, R. 2007. *America, Amerikkka: Elect Nation and Imperial Violence*. Sheffield: Equinox.

Sobrino, J. 2008. *No Salvation Outside the Poor: Prophetic-Utopian Essays*. Maryknoll: Orbis Books.

Sung, J. M. 2011. *The Subject, Capitalism, and Religion: Horizons of Hope in Complex Societies*. New York: Palgrave McMillan.

Taylor, M. L. 2005. *Religion, Politics, and the Christian Right: Post-9/11 Powers in American Empire*. Minneapolis: Fortress.

Te Paa, J. P. 2004. "Being Church: A Maori Woman's Voice and Vision." *In God's Image, Journal of Asian Women's Resource Centre for Culture and Theology* 23:2, 35–42.

Thomas, S. F., and A. B. Pinn, eds. 2010. *Liberation Theologies in the United States: An Introduction*. New York: New York University Press.

Tinker, T. 2011. "American Indians, Conquest, the Christian Story, and Invasive Nation-building." In *Wading through Many Voices: Toward a Theology of Public Conversation,* ed. H. Recinos, 255–77. New York: Rowman and Littlefield.

Townes, E. M. 2006. *Womanist Ethics and the Cultural Production of Evil*. New York: Palgrave Macmillan.

Walz, H. 2009. "Madres Appear on the Public Plaza de Mayo. Towards Human Rights as a Key for a Public Theology That Carries on the Liberation Heritage." *International Journal of Public Theology* 3:2, 164–86.

Yazbek, S. 2012. *A Woman in the Crossfire: Diaries of the Syrian Revolution*, London: Haus.

Contributors

Mario I. Aguilar, a Chilean by birth, is professor of Divinity at the School of Divinity of the University of St. Andrews in Scotland. His works include *A Social History of the Catholic Church in Chile* (9 volumes, 2004–); *The History and Politics of Latin American Theology* (3 volumes, 2007–2008); *Theology, Liberation, Genocide: A Theology of the Periphery* (2009); and *Religion, Torture and the Liberation of God: Liberation Theology within Globalization* (2013).

Thia Cooper is associate professor of Religion at Gustavus Adolphus College where she focuses on Religion in Latin America. She is the author of *Controversies in Political Theology* (2007).

Dwight N. Hopkins is professor of Theology at the University of Chicago Divinity School. He is the author of *Being Human: Race, Culture, and Religion* and *Shoes That Fit Our Feet: Sources for a Constructive Black Theology*. He is an editor of *The Cambridge Companion to Black Theology and Religions/Globalizations: Theories and Cases*.

Jeremy Ian Kirk is the PhD program coordinator and a PhD student of Social Ethics at Union Theological Seminary. His academic work has focused on exploring issues of complicity in systemic injustice; the future liberation theology; and the intersection of spirituality, performance, and social engagement. Jeremy has worked as an organizer with various environmental and human rights groups.

Wati Longchar is professor of Systematic Theology and currently serves as dean of SCEPTRE, Senate of Serampore College, Kolkata, West Bengal. He is the author of *Contextual Theology, Mission and Theological Education*, PTCA Series No. 4 (2012).

Sylvia Marcos is the director of the Center for Psychoethnological Research in Cuernavaca, Mexico. She is a professor and senior scholar founder and member of the permanent seminar Gender and Anthropology at IIA Universidad Nacional Autonoma de Mexico. She conducts research on the construction of gender and religion in indigenous, colonial, and postcolonial culture. Her books include *Taken from the Lips: Gender and Eros in Mesoamerica* (2006), *Religion and Gender, Third Volume of the Encyclopedia Iberoamericana de Religiones* (2004), *Women in Indigenous Religions* (2010), *Dialogue and Difference Feminisms Challenge Globalization* (2005), and *Indigenous Voices in the Sustainability Discourse* (2010).

Néstor Medina is assistant professor of Theology and Culture at Regent University, School of Divinity. He holds a BRE, MTS, MA, and PhD from the Toronto School of Theology, University of Toronto. His main areas of interest and research are liberation theologies, contextual theologies, and post/decolonial theologies. He has written several articles on these themes and is the author of *Mestizaje: (Re)Mapping the Development of Race, Culture and Faith in Latino/a Catholicism*, which earned him the Hispanic Theological Initiative Book award for 2012.

Ivan Petrella is academic director of Fundación Pensar and a professor at Universidad Di Tella and Universidad San Andres in Buenos Aires, Argentina. He is the author of *Beyond Liberation Theology: A Polemic* and *The Future of Liberation Theology: An Argument and Manifesto* as well as editor of *Latin American Liberation Theology: The Next Generation*, coeditor of *Theology for Another Possible World*, and co-executive editor of the *Reclaiming Liberation Theology* book series.

Mitri Raheb is the president of Dar al-Kalima University College in Bethlehem, president of the Synod of the Evangelical Lutheran Church in Jordan and the Holy Land, and senior pastor of the Evangelical Lutheran Christmas Church in Bethlehem, Palestine. Raheb is the author of several books including *Das Reformatorische Erbe unter den Palaestinensern* (1990); *I am a Palestinian Christian* (1994); and *Bethlehem Besieged* (2004). He is the chief editor of the Contextual Theology Series at Diyar including *The Invention of History, A Century of Interplay between Theology and Politics in Palestine* (2011) and *The Biblical Text in the Context of Occupation: Towards a New Hermeneutics of Liberation* (2012).

Joerg Rieger is Wendland-Cook Professor of Constructive Theology at Perkins School of Theology, Southern Methodist University in Dallas, Texas. For more than two decades he has worked to bring together theology and the struggles for justice and liberation that mark our age. A selection of his recent books includes *Occupy Religion: Theology of the Multitude* (2012, with Kwok Pui-lan); *Traveling* (2011); *Grace under Pressure* (2011); *Globalization and Theology* (2010); *No Rising Tide: Theology, Economics, and the Future* (2009); *Beyond the Spirit of Empire: Theology and Politics in a New Key* (2009, with Néstor Miguez and Jung Mo Sung); and *Christ and Empire: From Paul to Postcolonial Times* (2007).

Rosemary Radford Ruether is professor of Feminist Theology at Claremont Graduate University, Claremont, California. Her works include *Women and Redemption: A Theological History* (1998) and *America, Amerikkka: Elect Nation and Imperial Violence* (2007).

Malik J. Sales recently received his PhD from the Graduate Theological Union in Systematic/Philosophical Theology. His research interests focus upon soteriology, pneumatology, contextual theologies of liberation and resistance, and performance. Committed to creating variegated projects of resistance, Sales' future plans include publishing his dissertation, as well as producing a musical album and novel.

Charlene Sinclair is a doctoral candidate in Social Ethics and a member of the Poverty Initiative at Union Theological Seminary in New York. Her work utilizes critical social theories, empire critical biblical studies, and liberation theology to explore the intersection of social activism, social transformation, and spirituality. She also serves as the program director for Engaging the Powers, a program designed to train Black and Latino/a pastors in critical theory, policy, and strategy relevant to the development and implementation of social justice ministries.

Jung Mo Sung, a Roman Catholic, was born in South Korea, 1957, and has been living in Brazil since 1966. He is a professor at the Graduate Program in Religious Studies in Methodist University of São Paulo. He has written several books including *Desire, Market and Religion* (2007) and *The Subject, Capitalism, and Religion: Horizons of Hope in Complex Societies* (2011).

Jenny Plane Te Paa is an internationally renowned Anglican indigenous contextual theologian and academic leader who serves as dean at St. John's Theological College in Aotearoa New Zealand. She is one of the editors of *Lifting Women's Voices: Prayers to Change the World* (2009). bios.

Tink Tinker, a citizen of the Osage Nation (*wazhazhe*), is the Clifford Baldridge Professor of American Indian Cultures and Religious Traditions at Iliff School of Theology, where he has brought an Indian perspective to a predominantly Amer-European school. He continues to volunteer at Four Winds American Indian Council in Denver, an American Indian community project, where he has served non-stipendiary as director and as a traditional spiritual leader. His publications include *American Indian Liberation: A Theology of Sovereignty* (2008), *Spirit and Resistance: American Indian Liberation and Political Theology* (2004), and *Missionary Conquest: The Gospel and Native American Genocide* (1993).

Emilie M. Townes is the sixteenth Dean and Professor of Ethics and Society at Vanderbilt Divinity School. She has teaching and general research interests that focus on Christian ethics, womanist ethics, critical social theory, cultural theory and studies, as well as on postmodernism and social postmodernism. Her specific interests include health and health care, the cultural production of evil, and developing a network between African Americans and Afro-Brazilian religious and secular leaders and community based organizations. She is an American Academy of Arts and Sciences fellow, a former president of the American Academy of Religion (2008), and the current president of the Society for the Study of Black Religion (2012–2016).

Benjamín Valentín is professor of Theology and Culture, and director of the Orlando E. Costas Lectureship in Latino/a Theology and Religion, at Andover Newton Theological School in Newton Centre, MA. He is author of the award winning *Mapping Public Theology: Beyond Culture, Identity, and Difference*, editor of *In Our Own Voices: Latino/a Renditions of Theology and New Horizons in Hispanic/Latino(a) Theology*, and coeditor of *Creating Ourselves: African Americans and Hispanic Americans on Popular Culture and Religious Expression and the Ties That Bind; African American and Hispanic American/Latino(a) Theologies in Dialogue*.

William A. Walker III, is a PhD candidate at Claremont Graduate University in Philosophy of Religion and Theology. He earned his bachelor's degree in Economics and Spanish and his masters in theology from Baylor University. He is currently an adjunct professor of Christian Ethics at the University of the Incarnate Word in San Antonio, TX. His research interests include economic ethics, political theology, Latin American liberation philosophy and ecclesiology.

Heike Walz is junior-professor of Feminist Theology and Women's Studies, Department of Religious and Mission Studies and Ecumenics at the Protestant University Wuppertal-Bethel (Germany) since 2009. She was Extraordinary Professor of Systematic Theology at the Instituto Universitario ISEDET in Buenos Aires (Argentina) from 2005 until 2009. Her doctorate in theology (PhD) from University of Basel (Switzerland) was awarded in 2005. Her publications include liberation theologies, ecclesiology, women's theologies from the global South, postcolonial and gender theories, and intercultural theology; currently her research work is on Human Rights and Religion in Latin America.

Index

204   •   Index

d in the United States of America